"My Heart Is In the Cause"
The Civil War Diaries of Private James A. Meyers, 45th PA Volunteers

Edited by

Michelle L. Hamilton

MLH Publications
17221 Camellia Drive
Ruther Glen, VA 22546

Vanderberblumen Publications
P.O. Box 626
La Mesa, CA 91944

Library of Congress Cataloging-in-Publication Data

Hamilton, Michelle L.
"My heart is in the cause" The Civil War Diaries of Private James A. Meyers, 45th PA Volunteers

ISBN: 978-0-9644304-8-8

Special thanks to...

Anthony (Tony) Widmann

Tonia Falconer Barringer
(Niece of Anthony Widmann)

Sabina Widmann
(Daughter of Anthony Widmann)

*To all the family members who kept
these treasures safe for all these years*

*A special thanks to Sabina for asking me
to take your family story and bring it back to
life.*

Learning about one's ancestors is an experience unlike anything else in this life. It takes you out of the present, out of your own hectic lives to look back and identify with those who came before us. Each family member that can be singled out and brought to life through records, portraits and photographs adds to the fabric of our complex extended family. This fascinating window into the life of James Meyers is a welcome opportunity to relate to our ancestors and fuels the desire to learn more about the people who paved the way for our lives and the world we live in.

It is impossible for us to think about the Civil War now without thinking of our brave James Meyers who lived and breathed the experience. It is remarkable to see a member of our family in the context of this historical American event that truly shaped our country with lasting impact. A long and devastating battle that nearly broke up our new country, we salute James Meyers for his bravery and his willingness to enter into harms way in order hold our nation together.

We also salute our beloved Tony Widmann for maintaining the records and passing them down to the family.

I'm so grateful for Sabina's hard work and for Michelle's help on this project. How lucky we are to live in a time when there has been a renewed interest in family history, and where historical information is so much more accessible. I know I speak for the entire family when I say that we look forward to uncovering more stories and pieces of our family puzzle.

Tonia Falconer Barringer
(Niece of Anthony Widmann)

Picture of Anthony (Tony) Widmann

Introduction

James Alfred Meyers was born on September 10, 1841 in Lititz, Pennsylvania to Jonas and Sarah Hildebrand Meyers. James's father, Jonas Meyers supported his family as a tinsmith and later as a merchant. Unfortunately little is known about James's early life except that he had three older siblings: William H. Meyers, Edward J. Meyers, and Sarah A. Meyers. James's first appearance on official records is in the 1850 census where he is residing with his parents and siblings in Columbia, Pennsylvania. Ten years later in 1860, James had moved out of his parents' home and was residing with his brother Edward in Bethlehem, Pennsylvania. Edward was employed as a druggist and was teaching his younger brother the trade.[1]

The outbreak of the Civil War threatened to interrupt James Meyers's studies. Taken with the war spirit, James wrote an impassioned letter to his parents begging them to allow him to enter the army to put down the rebellion. Deaf to their son's pleading; Jonas and Sarah Meyers refused to let their twenty-year-old join the Union Army in April of 1861. By August of 1862, James could no longer wait for his parents' approval. A month shy of his twenty-first birthday, James enlisted in the 45th Pennsylvania Volunteers, Co. B as a Private on August 13, 1862.[2]

The 45th Pennsylvania was formed in October 1861 recruiting its members from Centre, Lancaster, Mifflin, Tioga, and

---

[1] Biographical information unless otherwise indicated provided by Ancestry.com.

[2] 45th Pennsylvania Volunteers, Company B muster roll, http://www.pa-roots.com/pacw/infantry/45th/45thcob.html, (online accessed February 10, 2015).

Wayne Counties. By the time that James Meyers joined the 45th Pennsylvania, the regiment had already seen action in South Carolina, Virginia, and Maryland. In 1862, the 45th Pennsylvania was organized as part of the IX Corps of the Army of the Potomac, commanded by Major General Ambrose Burnside. For James, his introduction to war came within a month of his enlistment at the Battle of South Mountain, Maryland on September 14, 1862. Two days later, the 45th Pennsylvania fought at the Battle of Antietam, Maryland. While the battle ended in a tactical draw for both sides, it proved to be the bloodiest days in American history. For the survivors of the 45th Pennsylvania, the Battle of Antietam was a defining moment for the regiment and a memorial now marks the spot where the regiment stood on the battlefield.

For James Meyers, his days in the front line soldier ended after the Battle of Antietam when he was promoted to medical corps as a hospital steward on September 22, 1862. James was promoted to this position due to his training as a druggist before the war. As a hospital steward, James became a warrant officer who ranked above the first sergeant of his company and was the only man permanently assigned to the regiment's surgeon.[3] In his capacity as a hospital steward, James was expected to "take exclusive charge of the dispensary, must be practically acquainted with such points of minor surgery as the application of bandages and dressings, the extraction of teeth, and the application of cups and leeches, and must have such knowledge of cooking as will enable him to superintend efficiently this important branch of hospital service."[4]

As a hospital steward, James Meyers served an important role in the daily life of his regiment and would be remembered fondly by his companions in the 45th Pennsylvania's regimental history published after the war. Private William A. Roberts of Company K remembered his wounding at the Battle of the Wilderness, Virginia, on May 6, 1864 and the role James Meyers

---

[3] George Worthington Adams, *Doctors in Blue: The Medical History of the Union Army in the Civil War* (Baton Rouge, LA: Louisiana State University Press, 1952, 1980), 67.
[4] Adams, *Doctors in Blue*, 67.

played in saving his life. "After resuming my position and firing three or four shots a bullet pierced my left arm near the shoulder and the Major ordered me to the rear. Just as I stepped back our line of battle came up and the engagement became general. The musketry on both sides was most terrific and the rebel bullets whistled around me like hail, cutting off leaves and branches. I walked back toward the field hospital as unconcerned as though they were so many bees. My only concern was about the poor boys who were facing that terrible fire, and whether I would lose my arm. Weak and faint from loss of blood, I came across a small stream of pure water and bathed my wounded arm. The sleeve of my blouse was saturated with blood. The application of cold water somewhat revived me and I proceeded on my way to the field hospital, probably a mile or so to the rear. The first man I met was our worthy hospital steward, Comrade James A. Meyers, who gave my wound some attention and stopped the flow of blood."[5]

2nd Lieutenant Ephraim E. Myers of Company K recalled how James Meyers cared for him after being injured at the Battle of the Crater (Petersburg, Virginia) on July 30, 1864. "When all was ready to move we were ordered to the right. We had not gone far in that direction when Captain Fessler gave orders, 'Close up, boys.' I repeated his command. That instant a cannon ball hit a tree and passing through, it struck me on the left leg above the knee. It was a spent shot or that would have been the last of 'Sweaty Myers.' Its force, however, threw me 10 or 15 feet. I landed on my back, down and out. Four or five of the boys carried me some distance to the rear. At first I thought my leg was broken, but it was not. It now grew dark. I said, 'Boys, go back to the company.' They told me two months later (when I had returned from the hospital), that they did not go back that night. The boys had laid me down in the woods. Our hospital steward, a sympathetic man, James A. Meyers, was always on careful look-out for any of us whenever the regiment went into action. He found me lying up against a tree, still holding

[5] Allen D. Albert, *History of the Forty-Fifth Regiment Pennsylvania Veteran Volunteer Infantry, 1861-1865* (Williamsport, PA: Grit Publishing Company, 1912), 115.

on to my canteen of coffee. The ambulance took me to the field hospital."[6]

James Meyers looked out for the members of the 45th Pennsylvania and was generous with his companions. Chaplain Frederick A. Gast recalled the time that James entertained him in his quarters in Burkeville, Virginia at the end of the war. Gast had gotten lost while traveling to Burkeville and had almost run into a band of Confederate guerillas. Upon his arrival in Burkeville, Chaplin Gast found his friend, "There I sought and found, James A. Meyers, hospital steward of the Forty-fifth. In the course of our conversation, I told him of my adventure and he informed me that, coming alone, I had been in great peril, for the country was overrun by guerilla bands. He entertained me that night and I shall always cherish pleasant recollections of his kindness on the occasion of my visit to Burkeville, as well as on some other occasions."[7]

The diary entries reproduced in this book where taken from two pocket diaries that James Meyers used to record his daily thoughts and feelings. James started his first diary on January 1, 1863 while the 45th Pennsylvania was in winter quarters outside of Fredericksburg, Virginia and concluded the diary at the end of January 1864. Unfortunately, the complete 1864 diary, according to family tradition, was destroyed by his aunts because of the graphic scenes James witnessed and recorded in his diary. This legend may in fact be true, as the 45th Pennsylvania participated in some of the Civil War's bloodiest battles. The second diary started on January 1, 1865 while the 45th Pennsylvania was engaged in the long siege of Petersburg, Virginia, the diary concluded on May 29, 1865 with James's joyful homecoming at the end of the war.

After the Civil War, James Meyers reentered civilian life and on April 23, 1868 married Anna M. Cowden remaining in Columbia, Pennsylvania for the remainder of his life. The couple would have three children James Cowden Meyers, Alfred Meyers,

---

[6] Albert, *History of the Forty-Fifth Regiment Pennsylvania Veteran Volunteer Infantry, 1861-1865*, 294.
[7] Albert, *History of the Forty-Fifth Regiment Pennsylvania Veteran Volunteer Infantry, 1861-1865*, 314.

and Maude E. Meyers. Despite witnessing scenes of unimaginable carnage during the war, James remained in the medical field working as an apothecary for many years. By 1890, James changed professions becoming President of the Columbia National Bank, a position he would hold until his retirement. Besides supporting his family in the years after the Civil War, James was also an active member in Columbia's Presbyterian Church. James was also active in veteran's organizations. In 1904, James represented the 45th Pennsylvania Volunteers on the Regimental Committee in charge of the Pennsylvania monuments on the Antietam battlefield.[8] The monument was dedicated at Antietam on September 17, 1904.[9] On February 23, 1907, James applied for a military pension, though it is unclear if he ever received a pension for his services.

On May 12, 1914, Anna M. Cowden Meyers died, following his wife's death James Meyers never remarried. By 1920, James was in declining health, succumbing to heart disease on November 4, 1920 in his Columbia, Pennsylvania home. James Alfred Meyers is buried with his wife in Columbia in the Mount Bethel Cemetery.

For years James Alfred Meyers's Civil War diaries lay forgotten, stored in boxes and passed along to the next generation as a remnant of the past. I had never even heard of James or his diaries until one day in the summer of 2012 when I received an email from Dr. Lawrence Baron, head of San Diego State University's History Graduate Department. At the time I was a grad student working on my history degree. The email was intriguing. How could I possible ignore a request from a descendant of a Civil War soldier who was looking for someone to help her transcribe her ancestor's diaries? I immediately contacted the current owner of the diaries, Sabina Widmann, and offered my services. Several months later in

---

[8] Colonel Oliver C. Bosbyshell, *Pennsylvania At Antietam: Report of the Antietam Battlefield Memorial Commission of Pennsylvania and Ceremonies at the Dedication of the Monuments Erected by the Commonwealth of Pennsylvania to Mark the Positions of Thirteen of the Pennsylvania Commands Engaged in the Battle* (Harrisburg, PA: Harrisburg Publishing Company, 1906), 233.

[9] 45th Pennsylvania Volunteer Infantry Monument, http://www.nps.gov/anti/learn/historyculture/mnt-pa-45.htm, (accessed March 18, 2015).

February 2013, I received an answer from Sabina asking me to come to her house to look at the diaries. Arriving at her house, I was graciously welcomed into her home and given the diaries to transcribe at my leisure. Sabina wanted the diaries transcribed as a gift for her father, Anthony Widmann, (James Meyers's great-grandson), and as a record for her children.

Transcribing James Meyers's diaries was an exciting and engaging project. For two to four hours a day, I was swept back in time and saw the war unfold through James. While transcribing the diary I became very fond of James and began to imagine what he looked like, for at the time Sabina did not have a copy of his photograph in her possession. I have to admit that I was a little sad upon the completion of the project, though proud that my work allowed Sabina and her family to get acquainted with their long lost ancestor. A few months after completing the project, I received an email from Sabina that her father Anthony Widmann had passed away. Fortunately, before his death he had gotten a chance to look over the transcription of James Meyers diaries. With Anthony's death, Sabina inherited the family papers, including photographs of James Meyers, his wife Anna Cowden Meyers, and his two sons. I was finally able to look at the face of the man that I had become acquainted with. I was pleasantly surprised to see that the man that I had imagined matched the face that was staring back at me.

James Alfred Meyers was a regular young man who answered his country's call. He served honorably and diligently cared for his comrades. To occupy his time, he recorded his experiences in small pocket diaries that were small enough to slip into his haversack. Though I have a feeling that James would object to me calling him a hero, I will anyway. He was a brave young man who followed the dictates of his conscience to fight for his country and for a cause that he believed in with all his heart. I am immensely grateful that he decided to record his daily life in camp and in battle.

I have reproduced the entries as they were written by James Meyers including the original spelling and punctuation. Occasionally I was unable to transcribe a word or phrase, which I have noted as such: [illegible]. Meyers frequently referenced his fellow soliders in the 45th Pennsylvania, fortunately the muster rolls for the regiment are available and I have included the information supplied in the muster rolls on his comrade in arms. The muster roll can be viewed online at http://www.pa-roots.com/pacw/infantry/paregimentsnew1.html. Below I have included a list of the engagements the 45th Pennsylvania was engaged in during James Meyers's period of service.

45th Pennsylvania Volunteers Engagements 1862-1865:

- Battle of South Mountain, Maryland, September 14, 1862
- Battle of Antietam, MD, September 16-17, 1862
- Battle of Fredericksburg, Virginia, December 12-15, 1862
- Siege of Vicksburg, Mississippi, June 14-July 4, 1863
- Siege of Jackson, MS, July 10-17, 1863
- Battle of Blue Springs, Tennessee, October 10, 1863
- Battle of Lenoir's Station, November 14-15, 1863
- Battle of Campbell's Station, November 17-December 4, 1863
- Siege of Knoxville, TN, December 5-24, 1863
- Battle of the Wilderness, VA, May 5-7, 1864
- Battle of Spotsylvania Courthouse, VA, May 8-21, 1864
- Battle of North Anna, VA, May 23-26, 1864
- Battle of Totopotomoy, VA, May 28-31, 1864
- Battle of Cold Harbor, VA, June 1-12, 1864
- Siege of Petersburg, VA, June 16, 1864—April 2, 1865
- Battle of the Crater, VA, July 30, 1864
- Battle of Weldon Railroad, August 18-21, 1864
- Battle of Poplar Springs Church, VA, September 29—October 2, 1864
- Battle of Peeble's Farm, VA, October 1, 1864
- Battle of Boydton Plank Road/Hatcher's Run, VA, October 27-28, 1864
- Battle of Fort Stedman, VA, March 25, 1864
- Assault on and fall of Petersburg, VA, April 2, 1865
- Grand Review of the Army, Washington, DC, May 23, 1865

- Regiment mustered out of service, July 17, 1865

Regimental Losses:

- In battle: 13 Officers and 214 Enlisted men
- From disease: 252
- Total: 479

Monument to honor the 45th Pennsylvania

Located at the Antietam Battlefield

Letter: James A. Meyers to
Jonas and Sarah Meyers

Bethlehem, April 18th 1861

Dear Parents[10]

Sister Sallie's[11] affectionate letter of this day came to hand a few minutes since. It was with deep emotions of pain I received the refusal of your consent to join the volunteers, to fight for my country and my country's flag, many of my young friends and acquaintances are in ranks, young men of good character and standing. Fred Frueauff last night came to join the company. Orville Ginder is also in rank. Our best citizens urge them on in the cause, and a large fund has been raised for support of families, and outfit of clothing for the men.

Many have good situations & homes, kind friends and relatives. Our company leaves tomorrow with about 80 men. Fred Frueauff is 2nd Lieutenant, the great feeling is manifested by all classes. Why should I remain when so many go? The necessity is great, and I can only with great difficulty remain from accompanying these gallant fellows tomorrow. I know my going will be hard on you all, but have not all the rest got just the same to go through, every one says to me why don't you go my name was on the list, but I withdrew preferring to wait, while you could be heard from—with the fond hope of a <u>Go and God bless you</u> from all of you heartily given, my heart is in the cause.

A second company is forming and I have promised be one of that number—consider well the matter—our all of country, home, & Liberty, is at stake. I am able and willing to go and do my duty as a

---

[10] Jonas Meyers (1798-1873) and Sarah Hildebrand Meyers (1801-1891)
[11] Sarah A. Meyers (1839-1890)

man. You will never regret your consent, and if I die, you will have the knowledge of my having done so fighting in a good cause, please do consent and let me go with a light heart knowing that those who are near and dear to me are with me in heart and looking with approving eyes.

As I said before my heart is in the cause, and your consent would be a great boon to me. We will be called out sooner or later.

Mr Dixon is very earnest in the cause, and contributed last night $5.00 to the fund, many gave $50.00 & quite a number gave $100.00, and are willing to double it.

Business will be suspended tomorrow morning, to allow every one to join in the [illegible] of our gallant men. A magnificent silk flag will be presented by the ladies of Bethlehem—, the great heart of the people is stirred and they respond nobly. Cannot our family be represented too not only by money, but personally.

Everybody strings out the Stars & Stripes and the town is all military, nobody can do a days work.

The excitement in the school is very great, especially among the Southerners, one of whom a Georgian today tore an American Flag in shreds, her sex was all that saved her from violence, her mother was the especial friend of James Buchanan when President, she was then Mrs. Craig, now Mrs. Robb, and I expect better of her daughter, who can now lay no claim to the title of Lady.

I hope all my young friends and former schoolmates who are able to do service, will be found in the volunteer ranks, and not wait to be drafted.

And now dear Parents I hope you will calmly consider this matter, and hope you may come to an affirmative conclusion. I do not, as I have told you, want to go without your permission, but the

15

case has become one of necessity, and by aid of a Good God I hope to come safely through, if He wills otherwise, I will say <u>"thy will not mine"</u> and hope to show myself worthy of the flag under which I fight.

You do not say whether my letter to Bro Will[12] was received or not. I received one from him last night. I hope to hear from you soon, and to hear too that your answer is Go! I wish I was home to see you all. Tomorrow, will some of my friends go, by whose side I promised to do battle for our country. I cannot do so but I hope soon to have the 2nd Company on hand. One of the volunteers said to me to-night, "Myers you can't go! But I glory in your Spunk!"

Write immediately. With much love to you all.

I remain your aff Son

Alfred

---

[12] William H. Meyers (1827-1874)

Part One: 1863-1864

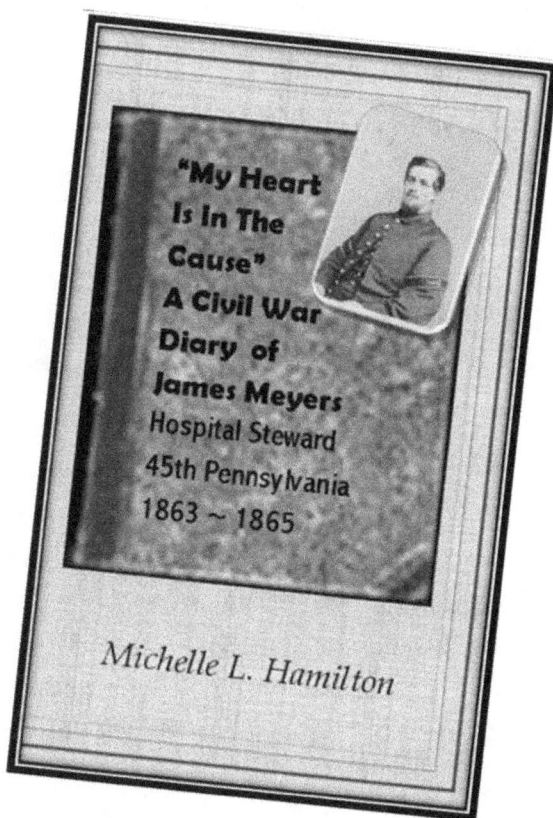

"My Heart Is In The Cause" A Civil War Diary of James Meyers Hospital Steward 45th Pennsylvania 1863 ~ 1865

Michelle L. Hamilton

James A. Meyers

Hospital Steward

45th Regt Penn Vols.

Of Columbia Lancaster Co Penna

Thursday, January 1, 1863.

The year 1863 opens clear and fine, I hope it may be auspicious of happy events in our national life. Our regiment, the 45th Penna Vols is still lying quietly encamped about one mile distant from Fredericksburg VA, directly opposite the city. The health of the regt is good and I have comparatively little to do.

Ev'g The day has passed quietly with me, with little or nothing to distinguish it from any other day. My friends Sam & Math have spent the ev'g with me talking over old times & scenes & bringing up sweet reminiscences of home & distant friends. The moon shines out clearly & the night is calm & beautiful, but some of the more turbulent ones amongst are riding a high horse, whiskey being on with out.

Friday, January 2, 1863.

This morning on arising I found that some one had during the past night entered my tent carrying off a demijohn containing some whiskey, which had been placed in my charge, also, had stolen half of our mess of baked beans

18

intended for this mornings breakfast, no clue to the perpetuator. But some of those who last night were drunken are now paying the penalty of their folly. Two Segts have been reversed to the ranks. Our Colonel is very severe on intemperance.

Recd by mail three letters & one paper, also this diary from Bro W—one letter from SW Knipe, W. tells me of good things from home on the way, how gladly we soldiers look for our mail with news from home & friends.

Saturday, January 3, 1863.

The fine weather still continues, 125 of our men are detailed for Picket duty. A very heavy hoar frost warns us of a change in the weather soon. Wrote to Bro Will. The letter from Sam K has given me much pleasure bringing to mind many pleasant thoughts of our boyhood.

Nothing of special interest occurred during the day in the evening wrote to Bro Edward, took a good old fashioned Saturday night's wash & change of underclothing.

Sunday, January 4, 1863.

Weather pleasant with a warm south wind.

Wrote to Bro Will concerning stove pipe which was omitted in the letter of yesterday.

Attended Brigade Service this afternoon. After a cloudy day we have a magnificent sunset, which was followed by quite a sharp shower of rain this in turn by a beautiful moonlight bright. This evening I received from Anne, Dress Coat, Boots, gloves & some Christmas cakes reminders of home enjoyments.

Monday, January 5, 1863.

Weather beautiful & Spring-like. Wrote to S.W.K.

Nothing of note occurred with us to-day. We are all anxious to hear [illegible] results of the last great fight in the west, Rosecrans comdg our forces.

Todays paper brings news of the loss of the Monitor with 21 lives, off Hatteras. [13]

The night is serenely beautiful, with an extremely bright moon.

This is the time to enjoy camp life.

Tuesday, January 6, 1863.

Sky over cast, commenced raining about noon. In the afternoon, our Corps was reviewed by Gen Burnside, the review was shortened by the rain. This evening brought another gorgeous sunset, beautiful moonlight and a sharp north wind.

Wednesday, January 7, 1863.

Opens clear and cold.

Wrote to Cousin C.E. Gidden—[illegible] Pittsburg Pa in answer to her letter of the 9th net.–

Nothing of special interest occurred during the day. The Pontoon trains & 50th Ny Regt Engineers removed from our neighborhood.

---

[13] The ironclad USS *Monitor* sank off Cape Hatteras, North Carolina during a storm on December 31, 1862.

Thursday, January 8, 1863.

Sky over cast with an appearance of snow. Recd our new medicine chest from Brig. Surg, much pleased with it.

It being Math C's[14] birthday we spent the evening together, talking of both past and future.

Sent my watch home for repairs, per WA Pfahler.[15]

Friday, January 9, 1863.

Still over clouded but not so cold as yesterday. Cleared off pleasantly. Took a walk to river bank and along our picket lines. A private (Wm McClellan)[16] of Co. E our regt was drowned in the Rappahannock about noon—he had been across the river & while returning the boat sunk. Was on picket duty at the time. Felt sick and in considerable pain all day, general feeling of debility. Recd in the ev'g by Express a Turkey & sundries from Home, two weeks en route & rather mushy.

Saturday, January 10, 1863.

Cloudy commenced raining about 10.30 AM & continued until after night.

---

[14] Private Matthew A. Cowden was recruited from Lancaster County and mustered into service on August 14, 1862. Cowden would be wounded at the Battle of the Wilderness, Virginia in May 1864 and was discharged on July 5, 1865. Information about the men of the 45th Pennsylvania Volunteers is based on the muster rolls for the regiment found at "Pennsylvania in the Civil War: Infantry Regiments" online at www.pa-roots.com/pacw/infantry/paregimentsnew1.html.

[15] Private William Pfahler was recruited from Lancaster County and mustered into service on August 10, 1862. On November 22, 1864, Pfahler was promoted to 1st Lieutenant and Quarter Master for the regiment. Lt. Pfahler mustered out with his company on July 17, 1865.

[16] Private William McClellan was recruited from Centre County and mustered into service on September 15, 1861.

At 6 am M.A. Walker[17] of Co 'A' died in hospital of Typhoid Pneumonia.

Sick all day, an old style bilious attack, took 4 Amp Carh Pills, which operated fully.

Sunday, January 11, 1863.

Rain ceased during the night. Sun is up early this morning.

I feel much better, but still have a headache, and a twinge in left shoulder something like Rheumatism.

In the evening received by mail, 4 papers, War Press, The Press, Inquirer & Lanc. Exam & Herald.[18]

Wrote home.

The [day] seemed very different indeed from Sunday at home. Scarce a thing to distinguish it from any other day.

Nothing of importance today.

Monday, January 12, 1863.

Opens clear and fine, very mild and spring like. Getting better and glad of it.

Jerome Scott[19] of Co "G" cut off thumb of left hand with hatchet. Dr. Christ[20] amputated the stump, & made a very nice job of it.

---

[17] Private M.A. Walker was recruited from Centre County and mustered into service on August 16, 1861.

[18] *Philadelphia Inquirer* and *Lancaster Examiner and Herald*

[19] Private Jerome Scott was recruited from Tioga County and mustered into service on September 18, 1861. On June 27, 1864, Scott was discharged from the regiment by Surgeon's Certificate.

[20] Dr. Theodore S. Christ served as one of the surgeon's for the regiment. Christ mustered into service on October 12, 1861. Dr. Christ was promoted to Assistant Surgeon on August 4, 1862, and was mustered out of the regiment at the

Nothing by mail.

Had my hair cut for first time since 18th Aug '62.

Tuesday, January 13, 1863.

Opens cloudy, still have sharp pain in head. I don't feel so well as yesterday.
5 months today since I enlisted in U.S. service, thus far all has gone well, at times all was difficulty & hardship, again all flowed as tranquilly by as if in peaceful times at home. Spent the evening with M.A.C, S.B.C,[21] SB.G[22] & J.S.B—.[23] going over old reminiscences & singing old songs.
Nothing by mail.

Wednesday, January 14, 1863.

Opens cloudy, damp and disagreeable. Feel almost myself again this morning.
Today made a checker board & played a number of games with different parties with varying success.
High winds in the evening, air warm & pleasant.
No mail.

Thursday, January 15, 1863.

Cloudy & windy, very warm for season, during the night the wind blew a gale, had to get up to fasten tent fly.

---

expiration of his term on October 20, 1864.

[21] Private Benton S. Clipper was recruited from Lancaster County and mustered into service on August 9, 1862. Benton was discharged on May 15, 1865 by Surgeon's Certificate.

[22] Private Samuel B. Garrigus was recruited from Lancaster County and mustered into service on August 13, 1862. Wounded at Jackson, Mississippi on July 11, 1863, Garrigus was transferred to the Veteran Reserve Corps.

[23] Private J.S. Brenneman was recruited from Lancaster County and mustered into service on August 10, 1862. Brenneman was discharged on June 7, 1865 by Surgeon's Certificate.

*In the evening received from home per WA Pfahler, $5.—
postage Currency, Postage stamps, Watch & note paper,
also learned of the illness & death of Aunt Pfahler at York
Penna.*

Friday, January 16, 1863.

*Open cloudy with some rain. We had another very windy
night with heavy rain after midnight. High wind still
continue. At noon we received orders to be ready to march
early on Saturday morning, busy all the remainder of the day
until late in the evg packing up.*

Wrote to Bro Will.

Dr. Christ left us early this morning on a 20 day furlough.

To bed tired and sleepy.

Saturday, January 17, 1863.

*Opens clear, calm and cold, almost 9 O Clock & no move
yet. The general inquiry is, Where are we going? Madame
Rumor, replies Washington, and again, across the
Rappahannock. It will hardly be the good fortune of this
Corps to get to Washington.*

*Evening, and still no move, I sincerely hope we may not have
to move in this cold weather. Recd by mail a letter from
S.R.G. Philada.*

*Our Dr. Styer[24] received his promotion to a Surgeoncy to-
night, ordered to the 179th Penna Drafted Regt*

---

[24] Assistant Surgeon Dr. Charles Styer mustered into service on August
1, 1862 and served with the 45th Pennsylvania Volunteers until his promotion to
Surgeon on January 12, 1863.

Sunday, January 18, 1863.

Open clear, cold, & calm. The past night has been one of the most severe I have experienced this winter. Had a full attendance at Sick Call Wrote to S.R.G—Philada—

Was very much surprised by a visit from Bro E.J.M.[25] who came to Aquia Creek to [take] Jas Leibert of 129th P.V. home on sick leave. Together with S.B. G—. we visited the river bank, batteries &c and took a look at Fredericksburg and the scene of the last fight.

Visited the Col[26] in the evening, & spent the remainder chatting about home and friends.

Turned in late at night. Report says move to-morrow. Wore my overcoat for first time this year. Weather has been so moderate.

Monday, January 19, 1863.

A very cold morning. Winter seems to have arrived at last. Bro Edwd left us for home this morning.

As the sun rose it grew warmer; and the day proved very pleasant.

This afternoon I discovered indications of my having the piles, my first experience in this line.

---

[25] The only trace that can be found about James Meyers' older brother Edward J. Meyers is an 1860 census entry from Bethlehem, Pennsylvania which lists his age as 28 and employed as a druggist.

[26] Colonel Thomas Welsh mustered into service on July 22, 1861 and served as the colonel of the 45th Pennsylvania Volunteers until his promotion to Brigadier General on March 1, 1863.

Spent the eve'g with Sam & Mark. Recd letters from Bro Will and SWK—.

Tuesday, January 20, 1863.

Opens cloudy but cold, indications of snow.

Christn Shank[27] of Co "B" teamster, died suddenly in the sink, & was buried this evening. The army is moving. The Left Grand Div moved past us today in a N.W direction. We have orders to move to-morrow.

Wrote to Cousin M.M.H. today Rain in the evening, which increased to a storm, at bedtime raining very heavily, a gloomy prospect for tomorrow's march.

Wednesday, January 21, 1863.

Opens with high wind and rain. A very severe storm raged during the whole night. The Regiment aroused at 3 AM for breakfast, all expecting to move but none made yet. (12AM) All is mud an water to day.

Various conflicting rumors are afloat, the storm continued all day & will very probably interfere seriously with the intended movement.

Recd by mail 2 diaries similar to this one, which I had written for, also some postage stamps. (Wrote to C.EB. Beth)

To bed early, a most disagreeable night and Sam is on picket duty along the river.

How fortunate are we to occupy our old camp tonight.

---

[27] Private Christian Shank was recruited from Lancaster County and mustered into service on October 20, 1861.

Thursday, January 22, 1863.

The storm continues, a fine driving rain, wind N.E.

A very large attendance at Sick Call. Wrote to Bro Will.

Visited Falmouth RRd Station in search of Express matter, unsuccessful, but obtained a number of delicacies for our sick, from the Christian Commission.

There was quite a large fire in Fredericksburg last night. From rumors to day it seem that we narrowly escaped having

another bombardment of Frdkby[28] the arrangements were interfered with by the storm.

Friday, January 23, 1863.

Opens cloudy, with neither wind or rain. A very busy morning, large attendance at Sick Call.
Sun came out pleasantly in afternoon, a welcome visitor. The troops which moved N.W. a few days since are now retracing their steps.

Saturday, January 24, 1863.

Opens partially clear, mild and pleasant. Peter Ross[29] of Co "C" died in Hospl—at 3. A.M. Typhoid Fever, later in the day the sun was warm and pleasant, but in the afternoon the weather was again overclouded.

S.B.G & I visited the RRd Station in search of our boxes from Philada friends, we were also at the Lacy House[30] &

---

[28] Fredericksburg, Virginia

[29] Private Peter Ross was recruited from Mifflin County and mustered into service on August 24, 1862.

[30] Chatham Manor is located above the Rappahannock River in Stafford

saw the earthworks in that vicinity. Could very plainly see the Rebel rifle pits on opposite shore, a mile or more in length, these Rebs are great diggers, returned at dark empty handed.

Sent all our sick excepting two from Hostl to Gen Hospl.

Sunday, January 25, 1863.

Opens damp and cloudy with rain before daylight, then sunshine followed by clouds, almost April weather. Attended Divine service in 100th P.V. in the evening. Recd War Press of 17th by mail.

Monday, January 26, 1863.

A pleasant day over head, but a sad one for the Army of the Potomac & especially our Ninth Army Corps, we lost our beloved Genl Burnside, followed by Sumner[31] & Franklin.[32] Truly a dark day for us things look dark and [illegible] for us to day. God grant us a ray of sun shine.
A letter from Cousin C.E.G—Pittsburg enclosing photographs of Wm & herself.
We had a rare musical break this evening, a brass band serenaded the Col of 46th N.Y. lying close by.

Tuesday, January 27, 1863.

County, Virginia. During the Battle of Fredericksburg in December 1862, Chatham was used as Major General Edwin Sumner's headquarters. Following the battle, Chatham was used as a Union hospital. Today Chatham Manor is part of the Fredericksburg and Spotsylvania National Military Park.

[31] Major General Edwin V. Sumner (1797-1863), commander of the right grand division of the IX Corps Army of the Potomac.

[32] Major General William B. Franklin (1823-1903), commander of VI Corps Army of the Potomac.

Opens with rain. Dr. Styer left before daylight, goes to join his regiment.

An Asst Surg of 100th P.V. attended our Sick Call.

Visited RRd depot again this afternoon, expecting one of our Asst Surgs.

A dull day throughout received the War Press of 24th by mail

Wednesday, January 28, 1863.

Opens with snow, had heavy rain during the night until nearly daylight. A hard night on our Pickets. Gave my revolver a through cleaning which occupied the afternoon. Wrote to Mrs Truman Philada in the evening. The day has been exceedingly disagreeable.

Thursday, January 29, 1863.

Opens clear and bright but the ground has a heavy covering of snow which nips the toes and reminds us of our northern homes.
The mail this evening brings me the "Press" of 27th.

Friday, January 30, 1863.

Opens clear and bright.
Had a visit from Offices of U.S. Sanitary Commission offering Hospl Supplies.
The mail to-night brings me a letter from Bro Will.

Saturday, January 31, 1863.

A beautiful spring like day. Visited the Office of U.S. Sanitary Commission and obtained a number of Hospital diet supplies. A busy day with me.

Sunday, February 1, 1863.

A fine spring like day with indications of rain which came in the evening.

Received letters from Bros Will and Edwd. The letter announced his safe return home. Also Leslie Illustrated[33] Paper and 2 gum Havelocks, one for Sam G & one for myself, fr Bro Will. Have had quite a busy day.

Monday, February 2, 1863.

Clear and fine, but cool and bracing. Busy with my patients, distributing freely the articles from Sanitary Commission.

Recd by mail a letter from Mrs Truman, and sent one to Bro WAM.

A beautiful moonlight night.

Tuesday, February 3, 1863.

Opens cold and cloudy, with a slight fall of snow after day light.

Called out on inspection at 9 A.M. in about a half hour the order was countermanded.

Sky clear at noon, sun bright & cheerful, but a strong cold northwind is blowing

A beautiful clear moonlight night, but bitter cold.

Wednesday, February 4, 1863.

Clear and very cold.

Mailed a letter to Sister Sallie.

---

[33] *Frank Leslie's Illustrated Newspaper*

Nothing of importance occurred today. I have quite a number of patients on hand, and succeed very well in my practice.

Spent the evening with Math C's mess & Sam G-.

By mail received a letter from S.R.G. Philada.

A cloudy night. Camp is full of smoke, indications of snow.

Thursday, February 5, 1863.

Opens biting cold with a driving Snow Storm, which changed into rain later in the day. 3.30 P.M. Col W— has just informed me that the 9th A.C. will go south, orders having arrived to that effect.

Spent an hour in the ev'g in pleasant chat with our Col.

The change in temperature has been great today, this evening the weather is warm and a heavy rain is falling.

Friday, February 6, 1863.

Opens cloudy & wet, the snow of yesterday has all disappeared. Visited Falmouth RRd Station in afternoon.

5. PM. Clouds are breaking & the air grows, a clear cold night freezing hard.

Saturday, February 7, 1863.

Opens beautiful & clear, yet mild, thawing the frozen ground & making muddy roads. Sent 3 men to General Hospt, Dr Christ returned to-night.

Spent the evening with M—C, assisted in putting away a can of peaches received from his home. Recd letters from Father & Cos Mary H.—

Dr. C—. brought with him the Regimental Colors which have been renovated & inscribed on them are James Island, June 10th, 62 South Mountain and Antietam, 3 engagements into in which it has waved.

Sunday, February 8, 1863.

A mild Spring like day overcast in the latter part.

Had a Turkey dinner furnished by Dr C-. Heard of the return of Genl Wilcox[34] to the command of our Div.—and read his Address to his command, was very much pleased. This gives great satisfaction throughout as the Genl is a favorite & deserves our esteem. If Genl. Burnside is returned to us we will be commanded as of old.

Monday, February 9, 1863.

A mild but over clouded day with indications of rain.

Wrote to SRG—. & inclosed a copy of Gen Wilcox's Genl Orders No 1.

Tuesday, February 10, 1863.

An extremely beautiful day, clear, mild & spring-like. At 11 AM received hurried marching orders, all bustle & soon in readiness.

The whole Brigade & baggage was at RRd before 3 P.M, the 36 Mass was shipped first & finally our own with the 100th

---

[34] Brevet Major General Orlando B. Wilcox (1823-1907), commander 1st Division, IX Corps.

P.V. followed, reached Aquia early in the evening, and after much bustle over regiment & baggage was loaded on the Jno A Warner, a boat formerly of Philada. Passed a tolerably comfortable night on the lower deck, amongst a crowd of our men. My position was much the shape of an S.

Wednesday, February 11, 1863.

Opens clouded & chilly, with a sprinkle of snow, then rain & then hail, with rain, making it very unpleasant on deck. We moved from Aquia dock about 5 A.M. steaming down the river, the river was rather uninteresting, the character of the shores was undulating, the Virginia side was sharp & steep, frequently covered by low pines. Shortly after noon we ran into harbor at St. Mary's river, dropped anchor, on account of storm on the bay which is yet 15 miles distant.

Here our cook went ashore and made coffee. Oyster boats came alongside selling oysters just caught. The boys were full of fun, making the boat ring in the spirit. I noticed a peculiar sort of fish resembling a sort of [illegible] with a red centre swimming around the boat. Made myself a more comfortable bed & turned in early with headache.

Thursday, February 12, 1863.

Opens cloudy with a little rain. Weighed anchor at 8.30 AM started down the river & in a little more than an hour were in the Bay. Although the wind was quite fresh the passage was smooth & pleasant. Saw great numbers of Wild Ducks, & Seagulls, the latter followed the boat picking up stray morsels. Spent most of the day on the upper deck watching each new point as seen. Pt. Lookout[35] was plainly insight.

---

[35] Notorious Union prison used to house Confederate POW's, located on a peninsula formed by the confluence of the Chesapeake Bay and the Potomac

Saw number of lighthouses. The men are very lively & in excellent spirits, sometimes rather rough, cleaned the sutler shop. Shot at mark from the After Deck, &c &c. The motion of the boat was so gentle that no sickness was produced. Passed an oyster fleet & saw one fishing. Have in sight of Ft Monroe[36] about sundown, to late to see much, run in close to shore & anchored. Hampton Village is but a short distance ahead. A noisy night, sharp storm of wind & rain at midnight.

Friday, February 13, 1863.

Opens clear and fine, cool & bracing wind. We are lying at anchor in the famous Hampton Roads.[37] The fort is on our Starboard. Hampton right a head & the Rip Raps (a low ledge of rocks) astern. Numerous craft are lying about us, but I can see nothing of the 5 [illegible] or Sylvan Shore with the remainder of our Brigade. I am enjoying my soldiers life heartily. Left Hampton Roads at 10.25 AM. Steaming up to Newport News, on the run saw a new monitor Battery firing at targets, also the wreck of the Congress & Cumberland.[38] Arrived at N.N at noon & by 2 PM has disembarked, met Drs. Hill & Shelmerdine of Phila on the landing. After considerable trouble succeeded in gathering all our luggage together. The Regiment went into camp about a mile from landing. Sent part of goods up, the remainder I remained with, in company with one of our hospital attendants. We

River in St. Mary's County, Maryland.

[36] Union military installation in Hampton, Virginia, several important military operations where launched from Fortress Monroe.

[37] Site of the Battle of Hampton Roads, Virginia on March 8-9, 1862, between the first ironclad warships the USS *Monitor* and the CSS *Virginia*.

[38] The USS *Congress* and the USS *Cumberland* where sunk by the ironclad CSS *Virginia* on March 8, 1862.

*made ourselves a bunk amongst the boxes & so passed the
night. The rats were very annoying here.*

Saturday, February 14, 1863.

*A beautiful clear day, late in the morning loaded up our
goods & started for camp, arrived about noon. After dinner
established our hospital & put up our other tents. I now
occupy one myself. Had oyster soap for dinner, quite a treat.*

*Our camp about a mile north of the landing, a four hundred
yards from the river, the location is fine, ground level, dry &
sandy. Our regiment was encamped very near here last
summer.*

*Orders have been issued to have the company quarters all
built alike 6 men in each mess, wide street &c, the men are
busily engaged in building & everything indicates a stay of
some length here. In the evening I wrote an addition to a
letter of 9th inst to SRG not before mailed. Also, wrote home,
and by mail received a letter from SWK.*

Saturday, February 15, 1863.

Opens cloudy with a slight fall of rain.

Monday, February 16, 1863.

Storm

Tuesday, February 17, 1863.

Storm

Wednesday, February 18, 1863.

Storm

Thursday, February 19, 1863.

Cloudy.

With a clear sunset.

Friday, February 20, 1863.

Opens clear and fine. Since Sunday we have an almost continuous storm of rain. On Sunday night I was taken with Bilious Fever & was confined to bed two days. When I was ready to be about again, my legs were completely crippled up, very stiff & painful. Having no fire in my tent I was very uncomfortable indeed. This morning I somewhat better and hope fair weather may restore me fully.

On Monday night I recd the long looked for express box from 10ᵗʰ & [illegible].

Saturday, February 21, 1863.

Opens clear and fine. Obtained a pass for Sam G- to go to Ft. Monroe & get me my stove pipe also same for hospital stove. Over clouded towards noon, wind shifting & by evening a cold north easter is blowing. Sam G— returned bringing the much needed pipe and to-night I am enjoying a

comfortable fire. Quarter Master McClure[39] returned to day bringing me a letter & pair stockings from home. I also received 3 letters by mail, a good day.

After dark the rain commenced and by 10 o'clock we were having a driving storm of snow & rain, a most disagreeable prospect.

---

[39] Quarter Master John McClure mustered into service on October 18, 1861; he was dismissed from service on September 24, 1864.

Sunday, February 22, 1863.

Opens with a powerful North East storm. Several inches of snow had fallen during the night and the ground is covered now.

Rain is falling in torrents every thing else almost is suspended. The snow is rapidly melting under the influence of the rain, my tent floor was covered with water at one time a complete flood is coming by after considerable I have drained off the water from the tent, but got drenched doing it. At noon the wind blew a tornado for a few minutes over turning a number of tents.

Monday, February 23, 1863.

A cold blustery day.

Received some dried peaches and silk HdKcf from home by Comm'y Sergt Roath.[40]

Tuesday, February 24, 1863.

Growing pleasanter.

Wednesday, February 25, 1863.

A mild warm day. Our Corps was reviewed by Maj. Gen Dix, it passed off very well, and the Corps presented an imposing spectacle, the time occupied was about 4 hours. I returned to camp very much fatigued & feeling the worse for the wear.

---

[40] Commissary Sergeant Jacob S. Roath was recruited from Lancaster County and was mustered into service on September 2, 1861. Roath entered service as a Sergeant in Company B, was promoted Commissary Sergeant on November 1, 1861. Roath was again promoted to 1st Lieutenant on May 21, 1865. On July 17, 1865 Roath mustered out of service.

By mail a letter from M.C. Felter Bethlehem.

Thursday, February 26, 1863.

Cloudy but mild & pleasant warm showers in the latter part of afternoon.

By assistance of Sam G- I have built me a bed stead with forked stakes driven in to the ground, and slender poles for cross pieces. Pine boughs for the mattress & altogether I will have an excellent bed.

I am still somewhat sore & lame, & feel the effects of yesterday's review considerably. A warm south wind is blowing and I feel exceedingly languid.

Recd a letter from C.E.B—. sun set splendidly.

Friday, February 27, 1863.

Over clouded but pleasant nothing of special interest occurred to day all goes on quietly.

Wrote to Cousin C.E.G—Pittsburg to day.

Nothing by mail.

My right leg is very lame again tonight, this Rheumatism proves troublesome.

Saturday, February 28, 1863.

The day opens clouded with a cool N.E. wind. This being the last day of the month, there is General Inspection it is also muster day. Four months pay is now due us. I was not present on inspection as my leg was very lame.

About the middle of the afternoon rain commenced falling & gives promise of another severe storm.

By mail I received letters from Bro E.TM & Sister Sallie, also the Tri Weekly Press. Of 24th & 25th inst.

Wrote to SW Kipe Columbia.

Sunday, March 1, 1863.

Opens cloudy & chilly, the rain has ceased but a high wind is blowing.

Took an inventory of Brig Medical Supplies for Dr—C. this morning.

Our Hospl Cook, S. Pettis[41] was discharged & returned to duty, a new one—Holliday[42] from Co H. took his place.

The change promises for the better. My legs are very painful.

Monday, March 2, 1863.

A very pleasant day.

I feel better today than I have done for sometime.

Our little Contraband Henry received a sharp cut with a knife in the upper part of left arm, at the hands of another of same color, the wound bled profusely but a compress and brandy stopped it.

---

[41] Private Sumner W. Pettis was recruited from Tioga County and mustered into service in Company G on September 18, 1861. On October 19, 1863, Pettis deserted from the regiment.

[42] Private Van B. Holliday was recruited from Tioga County and mustered into service on September 18, 1861. Holliday mustered out of service with his company on July 17, 1865.

Tuesday, March 3, 1863.

Open pleasant but a chilly wind sprung up in the afternoon, the evening beautifully clear & moon-light, but cool.

My left foot became so lame & sore about 3 PM as to be useless. Applied a woolen bandage [illegible] with Sol [illegible]. Am using [illegible] a mixture. [Sentence illegible].

Our new Asst Surg. Dr. Youndt[43] arrived at noon, quite a young man.

Wednesday, March 4, 1863.

The morning blustery & cold. My feet are much better, but I feel unwell otherwise & my bowels are constipated, for which I have taken a cathartic.

I remain close by my stove. By mail a letter & paper.

The night is beautifully clear & moonlight but cold, the wind has almost ceased.

Thursday, March 5, 1863.

Weather cold, left leg & foot continues lame.

Wind very changeable. The long on the road box from home arrived tonight most of the things on a damaged condition. Some entirely spoiled.

Friday, March 6, 1863.

Opens very cold.

---

[43] Assistant Surgeon W.S. Youndt mustered into service on February 23, 1863, he remained with the regiment until his resignation on May 18, 1865.

Another bilious attack. Scarcely able to attend Sick Call, down in bed again & took a through emetic. Which relieved me of much bile, after which I felt better.

Mrs Col Welsh, daughter Lill & Mrs. Wicke of Cola[44] arrived today.

Weather much moderate by evening.

Saturday, March 7, 1863.

Weather mild & pleasant. I feel much better this morning. Spent several hours this afternoon in conversation with Mrs. Welsh, learning something of friends at home.

Towards evening a heavy shower of rain arose.

Commenced & partially finished a letter to Bro E.T.M.

Sunday, March 8, 1863.

Opens clouded with rumbling thunder to the North West, and by 8 A.M. we had a sharp fall of rain accompanied by an occasional flash of lighting and clap of thunder, the first of the season. This in a few hours passed by and by 11 AM the sun shone clearly.

In company with Sam G- I took a walk along the beach the first since here, the sun was quite warm.

In the evening wrote to S.R.G. By mail received the Tri Weekly Press & a letter from WHM.

---

[44] Columbia, Pennsylvania.

Monday, March 9, 1863.

Opens with rain, which ceased by 7 AM & in a few hours the sun came out pleasantly. With Sam G— I visited Fortress Monroe in the afternoon. Going & returning in the steamer Geo Washington. Did not get inside the fort but went through the town outside. Saw the famous monster gun, named "Lincoln" it stands alone outside the fort in a small [illegible] battery.

The exterior of the fort presents a fine appearance, the massive walls surrounded by a wide moat seem impregnable.

Purchased a new cap & several small articles. Also had my hair cut & side whiskers shaved. The first shaving since out.

From the steamer got quite a good view of the Rip Raps & saw Sewalls point in the distance. Returned to camp at sunset, walking from the landing on the sand along the beach, the tide being out. Well pleased but quite fatigued with my trip.

Tuesday, March 10, 1863.

Opens chilly with a North East wind, which by 10 AM brought rain, which continued until evening, making an exceedingly disagreeable day. Nothing of importance today. By mail, the War Press.

My health seems to be rapidly improving. Appetite growing normal, my supper this evening was the only hearty meal I have eaten since our arrival here.

Wednesday, March 11, 1863.

Opens with rain, which from appearances has been falling heavily throughout the night.

42

This morning the storm is from the North West. Cold raw, & disagreeable, sun shine will be welcome.

The present storm seems particularly changeable the weather for the past two months has been very variable. Changing from one extreme to the other.

By noon the sun shone out from among the clouds, but the wind remains cold and increasing as the day advanced.

In the afternoon the 8th Mich Regt was presented with a new flag. Our whole division was out and after the presentation passed in review before Gen Wilcox.

Thursday, March 12, 1863.

Opens cold and bright, the wind strong from the N.W.

In the afternoon the sky was much overcast with heavy rain clouds.

Kept close to my quarters & warm stove. I am now almost if not entirely well again, appetite good.

Recd by two papers that had been ten days on the road, rather old news.

A few scattering snowflakes fell toward evening.

Friday, March 13, 1863.

Opens clear, bright and cold. Four men discharged for disability left this morning. A very strong N.W. wind made all shiver through the day.

At last when the winter is almost gone we are having a cook house built, the Pioneers[45] have been at work all day at it.

Nothing by mail except the Tri Weekly Press.

Today completes the first month of our stay here. We are enjoying oysters, they are plenty at from 20 to 25¢ a quart.

Saturday, March 14, 1863.

Opens bright with a South West wind, which soon brought clouds & promises to repeat our regular Saturday nights rain. Our cook house was finished today, a real sunny affair.

Had a game of football the first for many years, enjoyed it much.

For some unexplained reason our Commissary stopped the issue of Soft Bread & we are now on Hard Tack again. This may indicate a move is prospect. Our Colonel was yesterday

confirmed a Brig Gen by the U.S. Senate. So says a private telegram.

Surely the stars cannot be placed on a more worthy man's shoulders, though we shall miss him much yet I rejoice in his confirmation and say success to Gen Welsh—

Sunday, March 15, 1863.

Opens cloudy with a N.E- wind, another storm is prospect. Recd a letter from Bro. E.TM & wrote a hasty reply.

About 9 PM commenced raining heavily. Nothing of special interest occurred today.

Monday, March 16, 1863.

---

[45] Union soldiers detailed to cut roads, repair railroad bridges and works, and to dismantle enemy fortifications.

Opens cloudy with a fine driving rain from N.E. wind shifted to north & rain ceased.

Wrote to & received a letter from Bro WHM—

Tuesday, March 17, 1863.

St. Patrick's day opens fine but with a heavy frost. The day passed without rain being moderate & pleasant, an extremely unusual occurrence.

Received my sash from the Q-M. but no sword.

This evening received orders to be in readiness to march.

Numerous promotions have been made in the Regt. During the past few days. Quite a number from the ranks to commissions.

Wednesday, March 18, 1863.

Clouded with variable wind & some rain showers. Col. Welsh left on leave today Mrs. Welsh & daughter also started for home.

Evening, the air is full of marching rumors. Some say early tomorrow. I am in partial readiness. Orders have been issued for 5 days rations, our destination is unknown to us, but supposed to be either Norfolk or Suffolk, in this we may be sadly disappointed. We will leave comfortable quarters & with reluctance though camp life is wearisome.

Recd a letter from Bro WHM.

Thursday, March 19, 1863.

Opens cloudy with appearance of storm from N.E. The past night was one of busy preparation, company cook busy, orders for 5 days rations ahead have been recd.

One regiment (the 100th P.V.) of our Brigade made an early start moving towards Hampton by land. Our journey will evidently be a long one, rumor says to reinforce Rosecrans,[46] one thing is certain we are to go to Baltimore by transports. I have been very busily engaged in packing up today, have both Regimental & Brigade supplies to look after. We are back to Hard Tack again, old & mushy. Some that had been on the Peninsula.[47]

The Brigades on our right have moved down to Newport News there to embark. The day has proved very stormy, the

latter part of the morning sleet, then snow, which by evening was quite deep, presenting more the aspect of winter than spring, thus for our experience of the Sunny South has been unfavorable.

Wrote to WHM & ETM

Friday, March 20, 1863.

The snow storm continues, with little appearance of cessation. This must delay our movement some days. The past night has been a terrible one for those exposed to the storm.

---

[46] Major General William Rosecrans (1819-1898), commander of the XIV Corps which was designated as the Army of the Cumberland in 1862.

[47] In March 1862, Union Major General George B. McClellan (1826-1885) led the Army of the Potomac on the Peninsula Campaign to capture the Confederate capital in Richmond, Virginia. The Peninsula Campaign ended in failure in July 1862.

The snow continued until evening, & altogether the deepest we have seen this winter, the high wind drifting it quite deep in some places. On one side of my tent it is fully two feet deep. On the level about one foot. With the exception of going out for wood I kept close house. Spent the evening very pleasantly with Cowden, Garrigus, & Co. Mess G, Co 'B'.

Recd a letter from S.W.K—. The storm has prevented our moving, as it looks now we will scarcely leave before Monday or Tuesday next.

Saturday, March 21, 1863.

Opens with a cold rain from N.E. which continued all day, the snow disappearing rapidly before it.

No move yet.

Sunday, March 22, 1863.

Opens with a drizzling rain, about 9 AM, the sun shone out warm & bright.

All quiet until shortly afternoon when the order to move was received & soon our camp presented the appearance of a ruined town, marched to Newport News landing and shipped on board the steamer Mary Washington, Capt Cropper. On this boat the famous Capt Thomas Alias the French Lady was captured.[48] Our sick were all accommodated with berths, very comfortable, the regiment did not get on board until after dark, the baggage having been shipped first.

---

[48] Captain Thomas, known as "The French Lady," was wanted for piracy after seizing the steamer *St. Nicholas*. Thomas was captured on the steamer *Mary Washington* in July 1861.

Spent a very comfortable night although very warm.

Monday, March 23, 1863.

Opens mild & pleasant, under way at 6 A.M. Steamed down the James River & then up the bay.

The bay was very calm & the run quiet with nothing special occurring. In a few hours we passed the "Kennebec" which had an hour start of us, with the 36th Mass on board. A great number of small craft were plying & occasionally a large steamer was to be seen.

At Fortress Monroe we were stopped by a small tray boat which brought our captain his orders. At 9.45 PM landed at Locust Point opposite Baltimore.

No orders to disembark so turned in for the night & slept very comfortably.

Tuesday, March 24, 1863.

Opens cloudy, with a damp chilly wind. Up at 6 AM. Our consort the "Kennebec" arrived at 2 AM, from the deck can see 'Federal Hill' & fortifications, & various prominent points about Baltimore.

After considerable trouble & delay both baggage & men were loaded on the cars of the Balto & Ohio RRd. Did not begin to move until 1.30 P.M, after passing through the outskirts of the city we steamed along the Patapsco passing many splendid factories & mills possessing exceedingly good water power. Along the way we were cheered everywhere by the people young & old. A strange sight to us who have been in a hostile country for 5 months past.

The ride was very interesting although the accommodations were not very good. I rode with the baggage.

At Baltimore whiskey had rather the advantage of some of our men. Our landing place was at Locust Point. Stowed away for the night among the baggage & slept comfortably.

Wednesday, March 25, 1863.

Opens with rain. Awakened about half past four AM. At Harpers Ferry Va[49] where a cup of coffee & a loaf of bread was served out to each man. Again in desolate Virginia, mud everywhere.

The scene today was not very interesting, passing through a very mountainous country. Stopped at Cumberland Md for coffee. Quite a large old looking town, the road is guarded by Maryland & Virginia troops & one regiment New York soldiers.

By dark we were at Piedmont here the train was divided, the grade on the road becoming very steep. The latter part of the day proved very pleasant.

The night was not so comfortable as previous ones.

Our course lay close along the Potomac.

Thursday, March 26, 1863.

Opens on us at Grafton Va with snow, making it exceedingly unpleasant. Do not feel very well. Here we left the Balto & Ohio & took the N.W. V. RRd for Parkersburg. On this road we passed through 24 tunnels in a distance of 104 miles, making in all about 30 which we have passed through since

---

[49] Now Harpers Ferry, West Virginia.

leaving Balto. The country is exceedingly rough & wild. Coal mines & oil wells were plentiful. By 5 PM, we arrived at Parkersburg at the junction of the Kanawha & Ohio river & shipped on board the steamer La Crosse.

Feeling quite sick, bowls very constipated & symptoms of bilious attack. Through Dr C—. I was able to obtain a berth in State Room, took 4 Comp Carth Pills & turned in for the night. Passed a tolerably comfortable night.

Left Parkersburg at 10 PM.

Friday, March 27, 1863.

Opens pleasant, been underway for some hours, have come quite a distance from the Ohio.

Our destination is Cincinnati. Stopped at Ironton Ohio to board passengers, quite a crowd at the landing to cheer us on our way. Passed Portsmouth Ohio at about 1 PM. Took dinner in the Cabin, first meal eaten at a table since Sept 10th 1862.

Shortly after 5 PM. Passed Maysville Ky, quite a large town, with some fine buildings, were heartily greeted by the inhabitants. At 6. PM passed Ripley Ohio. The Ohio shore is lined with vineyards.

Arrived at Cincinnati about 10 P.M. The ride down the Ohio has been very interesting one.

At the towns along the shores we were heartily cheered, the ladies waving handkerchiefs & flags, all passed well.

Saturday, March 28, 1863.

Opens clouded & unpleasant. Shortly after day steamed across the river to Covington Ky & landed. This is a city of about 1700 inhabitants well built & paved.

Could see very little of Cincinnati, owing to the fog & smoke.

After landing marched to the depot of the Kentucky Central RRd Station & shipped on board the cars. At the RRd Station saw D. Peurt Erwin formerly of Columbia now of Cin—Ohio.

After some delay we started with all aboard and steamed away to the interior of Kentucky. The first part of the road lay amongst hills and through some fine country occasionally stopping at station or town. Among the towns were Cynthiana & Falmouth. In anticipation of an attack by Guerrillas all hands were loaded ready to receive them, but none occurred. Towards evening arrived at Paris Bourbon Co, where we halted & camped in the fair ground just outside of town.

The day proved pleasant.

Sunday, March 29, 1863.

Opens cold & uncomfortable. The night past was cold & clear. Slept in a large open building with a strong wind blowing through it, & caught a severe cold. After breakfast & Surgeons Call, went to work to arrange Camp. The men are all quartered in buildings, Officers principally in tents. The fair ground is large & fine, the surroundings country beautiful, the location would be a grand one for a permanent Camp.

The town of Paris presents evidences of wealth and refinement, many beautiful & large buildings are to be seen.

In the evening attended the Methodist Church in town, heard a sermon from 1. Cor. 13. 13.[50]

More than one hundred of our men were present, the night was clear & moonlight. Returned to camp to find my stove thrown over, tent had been on fire, little damage. Saved by Dr C— & Uncle Joe.

Monday, March 30, 1863.

Opens cloudy with indications of storm, growing pleasant later in the day.

Visited Paris in the afternoon & had boot mended.

Conversed with a number of Citizens. Some are loud in their professions of Loyalty, but many are open to suspicion, the population of the town is about 2000. A number of the citizens were present at Dress Parade & expressed themselves well pleased.

The Regiment went through the 'manual' by the 'taps,'[51] a new thing here, creating much wonder.

Tuesday, March 31, 1863.

Opens clouded with indications of storm. A hoar frost covering the ground.

---

[50] 1 Corinthians 13:13: "And now abideth faith, hope, charity, these three; but the greatest of these is charity." (King James Version)

[51] "Taps" was arranged by Brigadier General Daniel Butterfield (1831-1901) commander of the V Corps, while stationed at Harrison's Landing, Virginia in July 1862.

At noon a heavy snow storm set in, accompanied by high wind. Thus far we have not been greeted by many indications of the geniality of the Sunny South, though the citizens tell us that this is unusually severe weather here.

I have been suffering from an attack of Jaundice for some days past, added to this a severe cold, & I do not feel very comfortable.

The snow storm was but short lived lasting a few minutes, a bright sunshine following, this occurred frequently through the remainder of the day. Our Paymaster Maj. S Errett arrived today, received 4 months pay up to Mar 1ˢᵗ 1863, $120.—wanted to send $110. Home but could get no [illegible].

The month of March goes out stormy.

Wrote home.

Wednesday, April 1, 1863.

Opens beautiful and clear, a real spring morning. Sold my pipe and tobacco to Geo W. Snyder.[52] I intend abandoning smoking altogether, on account of my health.

Two regiments, (21ˢᵗ Mass & 51ˢᵗ Penna) came into Camp ground yesterday, expecting us to vacate & move further up the road. But our Col didn't just suit and await orders from Gen Burnside. Meanwhile the citizens of Paris have asked Gen B-. that we be allowed to remain here, the express themselves highly pleased with our Regiment.

---

[52] Private George W. Snyder was recruited from Lancaster County and mustered into service in Co. B on August 18, 1862 where he served until his death on December 21, 1863.

Thursday, April 2, 1863.

Mild and pleasant with high wind, quite unwell & remained closely housed all day.

Friday, April 3, 1863.

Opens pleasant, but proved a day of sunshine & storm. Snow, rain & thunder.

To town in the morning & sent to Bro. Will, by Express $100.00

Evening visited the Paris Cemetery, is very tastefully laid out and denotes wealth among the people here. A fine monument has been erected to the memory of the Bourbon Co volunteers who died in their country's service in Mexico. After leaving the cemetery took a moonlight stroll to town & heard some excellent vocal music accompanying the Piano. A strong reminder of Home. Enjoyed the walking much.

Saturday, April 4, 1863.

Opens beautifully clear and bright. Busy around quarters cleaning up & setting in order.

To town again at night for an hour, had a capital oyster stew with Com- Sergt Roarth, and was favored by some excellent vocal & instrumental music by our hostess.

The country round about supplies us with eggs, fowls, pastry &c in plenty at quite reasonable rates, eggs selling at 10¢ but have advanced to 15 @ 20.

Sunday, April 5, 1863.

Easter—. A real spring day, not a cloud visible, the sun warm. Had Regimental Inspection at 8.30 AM, after which attended Methodist Church in town. Sermon by Revd Perry, congregation two thirds soldiers. Religious services by the same in Camp at 3.30 P.M. Dress Parade at 5 P.M- out for first time. Our Camp visited by a large number of Ladies & Gentlemen.

In the evening attended the Reformed Church and heard an excellent sermon.

This has been more like Sunday than any day I have seen in 8 months.

Had a good supply of eggs for Easter, mush & milk for supper quite a rarity.

Having a permanent pass I am not stopped by the guard & go & come at pleasure.

Monday, April 6, 1863.

Opens damp and cloudy. Had a fall of rain during the past night.

An unsuccessful attempt at fishing, a stroll through the fields over an old camp ground and into an old family burying ground containing among others, the remains of an Associate Judge of the U.S. Supreme Court, of the time of

Jno. Q. Adams, I passed away the afternoon, the day grew colder as it advanced & the evening is quite cold & raw.

Wrote to L.S.L- & E.T.M. We are anxiously awaiting a mail, have received none since leaving Newport News.

55

Tuesday, April 7, 1863.

A clear spring day, somewhat cool but pleasant.

To town in the morning, had my boots half soled, and bought a new pair of shoes for $2.50. Got an excellent dinner for 25¢, returned to camp and found a letter awaiting me. Welcome news, the first since leaving Virginia.

In the evening walked out the turnpike to the Picket.

Another mail this evening by which I received two old newspapers.

Learned by today's paper that Brig Gen Welsh had been ordered to report to Maj Gen Burnside.

The night is cold and freezing

Wednesday, April 8, 1863.

Another beautiful day.

A sudden order from the Commander of Post for the Regt to report for military duty at 2 P.M. proved only to mean a Brigade Drill.

Attended the funeral of a Kentucky Soldier belonging to this vicinity. Services in the Reformed Church, interment in the cemetery adjoining our Camp, the firing party consisted of a detail of our men.

To town twice today, no sick in Hospital & my duties are very light.

Thursday, April 9, 1863.

Weather as yesterday.

About noon received orders to be ready to move, to rejoin our Brigade at Camp Dick Robinson. Avoided the final order to break camp until evening but none came.

Went to town in evening and attended prayer meeting in the Methodist Church.

Friday, April 10, 1863.

Opens overcast. About 2 AM was attacked by bilious diarrhea, and feel quite unwell from its effects.

Broke camp and shipped on board cars, by noon, we were at the city of Lexington. Saw the monument to the memory of Henry Clay, leaving Lexington and passing through a very rich & fertile country, seeing numerous fine residencies. Some very large orchards & vineyards. We arrived at Nicholasville the termination of the RRd.

Leaving the cars we marched the Nashville turnpike. After so long a rest the marching goes quite hard, the road was exceedingly dusty, & the wind driving into our faces, making things very uncomfortable. After a short march of about 3 miles we encamped for the night. Being fatigued the ground felt soft, and I passed a comfortable night, was not troubled with diarrhea after I laid down.

Saturday, April 11, 1863.

Still over cast, and quite warm. Reveille at 4.30 AM and shortly after Six we were en route our course is to the south or a little west of south, the high winds continues & drives the dust into our eyes. Having checked the diarrhea I march much more easily.

The turnpike is the finest I ever saw well graded & very smooth. Crossed the Kentucky river at its junction with the Big Hickman Creek, the scenery here is bold and romantic. The strata of the rocks lies horizontal in many places appearing like a wall of masonry. Should much like to spend a few weeks here, everything indicates capital fishing which I should enjoy. Continuing our march we passed through village of Bryantsville and about noon arrived at Camp Dick Robinson[53] where we again encamped, here we up with the remainder of our Brigade.

By mail received a letter from Sister Sallie. And per favor of Gen Welsh who brought them as far as Lexington, recd letters from Bros E.T.M & WHM & Sister. Also a neat photographic album from Sister containing her own, Bro Will's & SRG's photographs.

Sunday, April 12, 1863.

Opens cool, & overcast.

Today ends the 2nd year of war, how little did I think two years ago that it would last so long and that today I would be in Central Kentucky, a soldier in my country's cause.

A busy day arranging things around camp, opening our supplies, & issuing Brig Med Supplies. Shortly after noon Brig Genl Welsh came riding unattended into camp, but was soon recognized & heartily cheered, and welcomed, he seemed glad to be amongst us again, & I am sure we are to have him with us.

---

[53] Camp Dick Robinson, located outside of Danville, Kentucky, was the first Federal base south of the Ohio River.

Wrote a long letter to S.R.G—. in the evening & went to bed late.

In the afternoon explored a deep cave and spring on camp ground, the largest I have ever seen.

Monday, April 13, 1863.

Still cool & overcast, but cleared up towards noon & the afternoon was quite warm.

Put up a small Hospl tent, and have one patient, the first in Kentucky.

Made an inventory of Brig Med Supplies & unpacked them. Wrote to SWK. In the evening. Brig Gen Welsh assumed Commander of our Brigade today.

Tuesday, April 14, 1863.

Opens clouded, cool and raw.

Commenced raining about 10 AM. Nothing of importance occurred today.

Wednesday, April 15, 1863.

Opens with rain, a dull day. Co H. sent to do guard duty at the bridge over the Kentucky river.

A number of rebel prisoners brought in this evening.

By mail this evening received a letter from Bro Will dated 8th inst.

Thursday, April 16, 1863.

Clear and warm.

Lying quietly in camp.

Dr C—. absent for Medical Supplies.

Friday, April 17, 1863.

Clear and very warm.

All goes quietly. Quite unwell had an attack of dysentery with fever.

Recd by mail a letter from S.R.G— dated 12th & 3 papers.

Saturday, April 18, 1863.

Another clear day with a very warm sun, feeling almost summer like, making us seek the shade.

Am somewhat better, living on low diet.

Sun goes down cloudy with indications of rain.

Sunday, April 19, 1863.

Opens clouded followed by rain about 8.30 AM.

Recd by mail a Philada Inquirer of 14th inst, announcing the death of Dr J.H—Haskell on 13th inst. Dr H—. lived in 10th bellow Coates St.

Also a letter from Sister S.A.M. dated 12th inst.

Monday, April 20, 1863.

Clear and warm.

Our Brigade reviewed by Brig Gen Welsh in the afternoon.

Dr C—. returned, and our 2nd Asst Surg. Maxwell[54] of Armstrong Co Pa arrived.

Tuesday, April 21, 1863.

Clear and warm.

A busy day. Camp rearranged.

Heavy rain in evening & night.

Wednesday, April 22, 1863.

Opens wet, raining heavily, by 9 AM, clear.

A walk into the country in the afternoon revealed me some of the beauties by which we are surrounded.

Col Curtin,[55] was this evening, at Dress Parade, presented with a beautiful horse, by the Officers & men of his command.

Wrote to Sister SAM.

Thursday, April 23, 1863.

Opens with a strong west wind, partially clouded and quite cool.

Had fire in my stove, which felt very comfortable.

Friday, April 24, 1863.

---

[54] Assistant Surgeon John K. Maxwell mustered into service on March 3, 1863 and with the 45th PA until his resignation on August 27, 1864.

[55] Colonel John I. Curtin was recruited from Centre County and mustered into Company A on August 16, 1861 as a Captain. Curtin was promoted to the rank of Major on July 30, 1862. On September 4, 1862, Curtin was promoted to Lt. Colonel. Curtin was promoted to Colonel on April 13, 1863. This would not be Curtin's last promotion during the war; Curtin was promoted to Brigadier General on October 12, 1864. Brigadier General Curtin mustered out of service with his regiment on July 17, 1865.

Milder than yesterday, sun out warm & pleasant in afternoon. "Co E" was sent to Nicholasville to do duty there. Went to the Dick river on a fishing trip. Caught one "Striped Bass" a nice fish, the first of the kind I have caught. This river or what at home we would call a creek is a rapid stream hemmed in by steep limestone bluffs, the rocks in many places are perpendicular, the bed of the stream is very rocky.

In the woods along the bank Raccoons, Gray Squirrels & Wood Chucks abound.

Recd by mail, a letter from Sister Sallie dated 19th inst, mailed on 20th, through in 4 days, short time.

Evening cool & moonlight.

Saturday, April 25, 1863.

Weather pleasant, all goes quietly in camp, though indications of a move are increasing. Walked to Bryansville in the evening, a small village about one mile from camp.

Sunday, April 26, 1863.

Weather still pleasant, though cooler than yesterday. 37 of our men, from 'B' 'C' 'F' & 'G' under Provost Guard, arrested while absent from camp without passes last evening.

A 'General Inspection' in the morning, the turn out small.

Under marching orders, to move at a moments notice.

Monday, April 27, 1863.

Opens over clouded, but gives no rain.

By mail received the Press of 17th & 18th & 20th & 21st.

Tuesday, April 28, 1863.

Opens with rain, the day proves varied with sun & cloud, a real April day. Some thunder & lighting. Recd letters from Bro E.T.M. & SWK.

The officers of the regt had a ball at Bryansville the night was beautiful & moon light.

Wrote to Peterson & Bros Philada, enclosing $1.00 & ordering Dickens Dombey & Son & Pickwick Papers.[56]

Wednesday, April 29, 1863.

Sunshine and cloud, heavy shower accompanied by thunder & lighting in the afternoon. Health of the Regiment excellent, have very little to do.

Wrote to Sister Sallie and sent my overcoat and gauntlets home by express.

Thursday, April 30, 1863.

Opens clear & warm. Awaken by an early reveille and an unlooked for order to march at 7 AM. All bustle getting ready, but off in time, leaving Camp Dick behind we marched through a very beautiful country rolling and diversified by woodland. By 11 AM we reached Lancaster the county seat of [left blank][57] *County. Shortly afternoon we crossed the Dick river & halted for coffee, resuming our march we made Stanford about 5 P.M. & encamped about ½ mile outside of town, having marched about 18 miles, a good march for just fresh from Camp -.*

---

[56] *Dombey and Son* (1848) and *The Pickwick Papers* (1837) by Charles Dickens.

[57] Section left blank by James Meyers.

Our regiment stood it well but few falling out.

By mail received Harper's Weekly from M.E.H—.

Friday, May 1, 1863.

*May comes in beautiful and quite warm. Awakened early &
ready to resume march, but the orders were counter manded.*

*Wrote to Bro E.T.M & spent the morning reading, feeling
fatigued from yesterday's march, did move around much.*

*At noon received orders to march at 1 P.M. We occupied the
extreme left & did not get under way until 1.45 P.M.*

*By 6 PM we were at Houstonville having marched 10 miles
& encamped for the night beside a fine stream called the
Head of Hanging Falls.*

*Math C-. fell out for the first time, fainted & was much
exhausted, brought him up in ambulance & by bed time felt
better. Houstonville is quite a pretty village of about 1000
inhabitants.*

Saturday May 2, 1863.

Opens clear and warm.

*Tried fishing in the river & found it quite good, having the
same fish as our home streams.*

*Resumed our march at One PM. The country through which
we our now passing is more hilly than any part of Ky that we
have yet seen. Some of the scenery is quite beautiful. As we
advanced the land became less cultivated and fertile, but
after passing thru a belt of woodland with a ground
[illegible] we again opened into a fine country.*

64

We arrived at Middleburg about 6 P.M, & encamped on the banks of the Green River in a low damp meadow. Haversack empty went foraging without success.

All our Knapsacks were [illegible] & we marched rapidly, men & good spirits, felt very well after it. Middleburg consists of some three or 4 houses. We here leave the turnpike & take dirt roads. The night is cloudy & we shall have rain.

Sunday, May 3, 1863.

Opens wet. Some rain fell during the [night] & there is prospect of more. A family consisting of a father & several daughters, from Scott County Ten— came in today. They have a terrible tale of suffering & rebel barbarity to relate.

Wrote to M.E.H. this morning, also to Bro WHM.

A large sum of money was collected and handed to the Refugees.

Took a bath in the Green River, first swim of the season.

Laid quietly in camp all day, had some heavy showers of rain and towards evening a beautiful rainbow.

By mail received a letter from Sallie R.G-. through in four days also a paper from WHM.

Monday, May 4, 1863.

Opens foggy and damp, but cleared up very warm.

At noon packed up and moved camp to a more favorable location on high ground.

A heavy rain shower at 2 PM.

Fishing in Green River, caught some fish mostly small.

Tuesday, May 5, 1863.

Cloudy with rain. Still in camp. 2nd Brigade passed us in the forenoon. Considerable rain through the day.

Turned in my wall tent retaining only the fly for future use. Also sent my stove with other extra baggage to Nicholasville for storage. We are gradually coming down to active service.

Wednesday, May 6, 1863.

Still cloudy and getting cool. Nothing of importance occurring except news of the success of Hooker's Army at Fredericksburg. They are gladding to all.

Heavy rain at night.

Thursday, May 7, 1863.

The heavy rain continued and will effectively prevent our moving for some day the river is high & rising, roads muddy & sky promises more rain. Put up hospital tent & stove. Weather cool & unpleasant. The good news from Fredericksburg continue. Wrote to C. E B[illegible].

+ Late in evening Danl Glossner[58] Co 'D' was brought in with a severe wound in right arm caused by Frank Smith[59]

---

[58] Private Daniel Glossner was recruited from Centre County and mustered into service on September 23, 1861 at the expiration of his term of service was mustered out on October 20, 1864.

[59] James Meyers could be referring to Private Benjamin F. Smith who was recruited from Centre County and mustered into service on September 15, 1861 and on the expiration of his term of service mustered out on October 20, 1864.

also Co 'D' whilst intoxicated, the muscle & artery were severed, lost much blood, and had a narrow escape.

+ Saw this man again at Corington Ky in August 1863 after my return from Mississippi, the wounded arm was losing flesh and there was no probability of a recovery of its usefulness.

Friday, May 8, 1863.

Opens cloudy with drizzling rain. Clouds broke & cleared away about noon & sun came out warm & pleasant. News from the Army of Potomac not so favorable today.

Wrote to SWK.

Unwelcome news from Hookers Army.[60]

Saturday, May 9, 1863.

Opens clear and bright, recd by mail the books which I had sent to Peterson for.

Another mail in evening by which I recd letter from Sister S.A M.

Sunday, May 10, 1863.

Opens clear and warm.

The camp full of rumor from Rappahannock and Richmond. At sundown a dispatch from Stanford to Genl Welsh stating that Hooker had again crossed the Rappahannock & that Dix & Stoneman had taken Richmond, the stars & stripes

---

[60] Following Major General Ambrose Burnside's defeat at the Battle of Fredericksburg, Virginia, Major General Joseph Hooker (1814-1879) assumed command of the Army of the Potomac. The Army of the Potomac suffered a severe defeat at the Battle of Chancellorsville, Virginia (April 30-May 6, 1863).

waving over the Rebel Capital, caused great joy & shouting through the camps, making the old Kentucky hills ring with the cheers. God grant that it may prove true.

What a canard it proved to be, and how many of the brave boys whose hearts it gladdened them, laid down their lives for their Country's Cause long ere the hoped for event came, but come it did.[61]

Monday, May 11, 1863.

Clear and warm.

Marching orders at noon broke camp and moved at 2 PM. Marched to Houstonville, 10 miles & went into camp at 6.30 P.M.

Our location is near the ground occupied when here on 1st & 2nd insts.

The afternoon was very warm. The Division headquarters have been removed with us, and are now adjoining our camp.

The location is very beautiful a fair stream bounding one side.

Tuesday, May 12, 1863.

Clear and warm.

Busy in morning around camp, and in afternoon strolling around the creek, trying for fish but finding none.

We are again in receipt of a daily mail.

---

[61] This paragraph was added later by James Meyers.

Wednesday, May 13, 1863.

Rain, dull day in camp.

Thursday, May 14, 1863.

Clear & pleasant.

Friday, May 15, 1863.

Clear & pleasant.

Recd a letter from S.R.G. and wrote to SAM.

Saturday, May 16, 1863.

Clear & growing warm.

To Houstonville this evening.

Sunday, May 17, 1863.

A beautiful day.

Recd a letter from W.H.M. & wrote to S.R.G.—.

Divine service in camp by Chaplin Gibson[62] in afternoon, largely attended by citizens.

The night is quite cold.

Monday, May 18, 1863.

Opens clear & cool.

Received our medical supplies which had been sent for from Camp Dick Robinson, one month ago.

---

[62] Chaplin William J. Gibson mustered into service on October 1, 1861, and remained with the regiment until his resignation on January 1, 1864.

Repacked & condensed some of the packages.

The night is[63]

Tuesday, May 19, 1863.

Aroused shortly after 2 A.M. by great noise in camp, caused by preparation to march immediately. The regiment was on the road by 3 o'clock & was sent out in two detachments with artillery to receive our attack from the enemy. After much hurry the baggage was ready, then lay quietly by until about 8 AM. When we took the Stanford road & went several miles beyond Hustonville, about faced & back to camp again by 1 P.M. when we found the regiment in advance of us.

It all looks very much like a game of Gen Welsh's a sort of drill, all passed well.

Late in the day many of the officers attended a picnic near town.

Camp re established & all goes on as usual.

Wednesday, May 20, 1863.

A warm & dusty day.

Recd two mails one old & the other regular. A number of missing papers turned up. A letter from L.ST in evening.

S. Hinkle[64] of Co 'B' home on furlough returned, bringing letter from S.A.M. & SWK dated 17th.

---

[63] James Meyers failed to complete this sentence.

[64] Corporal Samuel M. Hinkle recruited from Lancaster County and mustered into service on August 1, 186-, died on July 1, 1864 from wounds received at Petersburg, Virginia on June 17, 1864.

Thursday, May 21, 1863.

Warm & dusty.

The citizens of Houstonville have through a committee notified us of a dinner or Picnic for the soldiers of our regiment, to be given on our grounds tomorrow.

Great preparations are being made for it.

Friday, May 22, 1863.

Opens a bright and propitious day for our picnic, the mail last night brought me an interesting letter from M.E.H, dated 16th inst.

Our camp is thoroughly policed, a table 175 yards [Sic.] long has been erected, and provisions & people are arriving rapidly. The line officers of the regt have relieved the pickets doing duty in their stead, rather a rare sight to see shoulder straps sporting muskets. The dinner was good & well enjoyed, plenty of it & all passed quickly & in decorum. As 2 PM. The speaking commenced. Sergt Hollahan[65] of Co 'A' opening, followed by Sergt Yarrington[66] of Co 'D' who preceded Col Wolford[67] of the 1st Ky Cavalry, an old Comrade in Arms of Gen Welsh's in the Mexican War & then by Gen T'ry, all able speeches, the latter lengthy & full

---

[65] 1st Sergeant John F. Hollahan was recruited from Centre County and mustered into service on October 20, 1861. Hollahan received his promotion to 1st Sergeant on March 1, 1863. On July 30, 1864 Hollahan was wounded at Petersburg, Virginia, he recovered and was mustered out on October 20, 1864 at the expiration of term of his service.

[66] Sergeant Abiel A. Yarrington was recruited from Centre County and mustered into service on March 25, 1862 and was mustered out of service on March 25, 1865 at the expiration of his term of service.

[67] Colonel Frank Lane Wolford (1817-1895), served as commander of the 1st Kentucky Calvary from 1861 to 1864.

of fire & patriotism, listened too with marked attention by all.

The whole affair passed off very creditable, & many were the praise we received for good conduct & discipline.

Saturday, May 23, 1863.

Opens warm and clear. Ordered to be ready to march at an early hour, but lay in readiness until 11 AM before we moved.

Then taking the Liberty turnpike we had a warm & dusty march to Carpenters creek, took coffee & leaving the pike we continued on our way over ordinary country roads. The appearance of the country grew rougher & the soil less fertile as we advanced but there were some beautiful scenes. By evening we made the Green river and at about 7.30 P.M. passed thru Liberty (County Seat of Casey Co'y) and encamped on the edge of the town, on a flat [illegible] a few hundred yards of the river.

The march was warm, but feeling well I came into camp fresh and nimble, the distance made was 15 miles. The remainder of our Brigade is 3 miles in advance, having left Middleburg to-day.

3 men from our Hospl were sent back today. Wrote a long letter to Sister Sallie this morning.

Sunday, May 24, 1863.

Another bright hot day, aroused early with orders to march at 6 AM. All in readiness and the men in line when the order was countermanded & now we wait. Orders countermanded and camp re-established.

Spent the day quietly in camp it being too warm to move around much.

Visited Liberty in the evening and found it a miserable place, the Court House & jail poor affairs indeed. The entire place consists of a few dozen indifferent houses calling to mind some of the Virginia towns as seen last fall.

This is the home of Col Wolford of the 1ˢᵗ Ky Calvary.

Orders to be in line at 6 AM tomorrow.

Monday, May 25, 1863.

Opens bright & warm.

In line by 6 AM, and as we are to be in rear of the trains and all, it will be some hours before we move. In motion about 8 AM but going slowly with frequent stops, followed the course of the Green river for some miles, noted some beautiful fishing spots evidently well stocked.

One of the wagon masters was knocked down & run over by the team & wagon, seriously injured.

Leaving to river we ascended a steep bluff, very difficult for the teams. After gaining the summit we had level but dusty roads for miles through a dense forest, meeting with but an occasional cleared spot, with a log cabin. Again descending from the ridge we struck the river & crossed. Continuing our way some three miles further we reached camp about sunset, having marched 15 miles, & feeling in splendid condition.

Considering the rough condition of the roads the teams made excellent time meeting with but few mishaps. The day was exceedingly warm & the roads very dusty.

Tuesday, May 26, 1863.

Clear and very warm.

Up early & marched at 7 AM. Continuing as rear guard for the whole Brigade & trains. Almost the whole distance was through a dense forest, giving us a fine protection from the sun, though there was but little air stirring. Had a good long rest & cup of tea at noon by a beautiful spring of excellent water.

Resuming our march we reached camp about 3 PM, & camped on high ground beside Russell's Creek about 1 ½ miles from Columbia, in Adam Co'y.

Had a good through march & arranged camp, feeling capitally.

The nights are bright & beautiful. We have rumors of a near proximity of the enemy.

Wednesday, May 27, 1863.

Clear and warm.

Indications a prolonged stay here are abundant. A general re arrangement of our camp, and through policing of the ground.

Russell's Creek has quite a good stock of fine fish, of which some of boys have secured a few.

The 100th P.V. & 36th Mass Regts, with 4 cannon, left this evening on a scout.

Two regiments from the 1st Brigade were also sent out.

They went in light marching order and may find work to do before they return.

Had a good swim in Russell's Creek, water about 12 or 15 ft deep & very pleasant.

Thursday, May 28, 1863.

Opens clear & warm.

Hazy about noon with indications of rain which we hope to receive, as 15 days have passed without rain everything is very dry.

Wrote to Bro WAM, and received a letter from S.R.G.

A shower of rain in the evening followed during the night by quite a heavy fall.

Friday, May 29, 1863.

Opens cool and pleasant after the rain.

Broke camp and marched about noon through Columbia towards Jamestown.

Heavy rain commenced early in the afternoon & the roads were very muddy, lay by in the woods until about 5 P.M. then marched until 9 P.M. over very rough roads & rough woods.

Camped in a woods near a church, which we used as a hospital. Slept comfortably on a hard bench with an overcoat for covering.

Columbia is somewhat larger than Liberty, but yet a poor excuse for a County Seat presenting little show of energy. Was very sick for several hours on the march, the effects of an overdose of Frich opium taken to check Diarrhea.

Saturday, May 30, 1863.

Up at 5 AM. Weather somewhat more settled, leaving camp we again took the rear of Brigade.

Sergt Yarrington & myself stopped at a farm house and took a good lunch of biscuits and milk.

The Brigade reached Liberty about 11 AM. And relieved the other forces there.

Had a heavy thunder shower in the evening.

+ Liberty is the county seat of Russell County, a small village with a brick court house in center. Many of the inhabitants have departed the place some going north & others south. Co 'A' is doing Provost duty & Capt Tyson[68] is Provost Marshal. Col Curtin commands the forces here, consisting of 17th & 27th Mich regt a battery of Artillery four cavalry & our own regiment.

+ Should be Jamestown—locally styled "Jimtown."

Sunday, May 31, 1863.

Opens with rain followed by some sun shine & then rain again.

The day passed quietly, not feeling very well took a dose of Margna Sueph which gave me a good physic. Another storm

---

[68] Captain William W. Tyson was recruited from Centre County and mustered into service on August 16, 1861. Tyson entered service at a 1st Sergeant, but was quickly promoted to 2nd Lieutenant on December 2, 1861. On August 17, 1862, Tyson was promoted to 1st Lieutenant, then on September 25, 1862 Tyson was promoted for the final time to Captain. Tyson remained with the regiment until October 20, 1864 when he was mustered out at the expiration of his term of service.

of thunder and lightening in evening the heaviest of the season.

Received a mail, 4 newspapers but not letters, one paper through from Philada since 26th.

Monday, June 1, 1863.

The first day of Summer opens bright, but proves a day of showers.

Wrote to M.E.H.

About noon the camp was aroused by the long roll and forces were sent out in different directions, everything looked like a meeting with rebels soon, but towards evening the troops retuned without meeting any foe.

Tuesday, June 2, 1863.

Aroused about 5 AM by the cry 'the Rebels are coming' followed by quick shots in rapid succession & the sounding of the long roll. All hands out, and an examination found that a small force of reb's had driven in our cavalry & infantry pickets in hot haste, causing a little skirmish near town with no loss. When the Rebs wheeled & retreated as rapidly as they came, one or two prisoners were captured & they carried off blankets &c belonging to the pickets.

The 36th Mass arrived just at the time, having marched from Cola69 during the night went immediately into line, the woods were searched. One party going to the bank of Cumberland river but the bird had flown.

---

69 Columbia, Kentucky.

Gen Welsh arrived later in the day. Our brigade is now numbered the 1st, commanded by Col Bowman[70] of the 36th Mass & consists of the 17th & 27th Mich, 36th Mass & our own—

Wednesday, June 3, 1863.

Passed quietly in camp with the exception of sending out Scouting parties & the arrival of several citizens nothing special occurred.

Thursday, June 4, 1863.

Opens warm and pleasant very unexpected orders to march were received and about noon we left Jamestown taking the Columbia road.

Marched rapidly, stopped at dusk to leave wagon train pass & made coffee, were much detained by the train & did not arrive in camp until quite late, feeling much fatigued.

Carried my blankets. Recd by mail two Philada Presses.

Friday, June 5, 1863.

Opens bright and warm.

Up early after a tolerably comfortable night.

En route by 6.30 AM. Taking the Lebanon turnpike & marched rapidly over an excellent road. Were somewhat troubled by dust. At noon crossed the Green river & halted for coffee resuming our march we reached Campbellville Taylor Co. at 5.30 & camped one mile beyond the town, having marched 21 miles or more.

---

[70] Colonel Henry Bowman, commander 36th Massachusetts Infantry.

Came in somewhat footsore.

Orders for Reveille at 3 AM & marched at 4 AM tomorrow.

Saturday, June 6, 1863.

Aroused at 3 AM, marched at 4. Weather warm, road dusty. After many apparently unnecessary halts we reached Lebanon between 1 & 2 PM. I much fatigued.

Camped on an extremely dirty ground near the RRd. Recd letters from S.A.M. E.T.M. & CEB.—.

Too tired to run around much so lay quietly by.

Our march in 48 hours was about 60 miles.

Pay master commenced paying the regiment.

The night was cool, slept comfortably

Sunday, June 7, 1863.

Opens cloudy & cool, busily engaged in morning getting ready for RRd movements. Recd two mo's pay to Apl 30ᵗʰ got a check for $80.—to send home $30 for SBG—. $50 for myself.

Broke camp at noon, marched to the cars, loaded, and left at 4 PM. After a fine run through a level & uninteresting country we reached Louisville at 8 PM.

Debarked & passed through the city ferried over the Ohio to Jeffersonville Indiana & shipped on board the Jeffersonville RRd.

The night was very cool, did not get loaded & fixed until 2 AM, when turned in and caught a few hours sleep among the brigade.

Louisville by night presented a fine appearance, took supper at a Restaurant, on Jefferson Street.

Monday, June 8, 1863.

Up at 5 A.M. Clear and bright.

Did not move until 9 AM considerable time being lost in loading the other regiments.

Crowds of hucksters with eatables of all kinds roamed around. We are already making the change from Slave to free Soil, which becomes more marked as we advance into the country. White labor superseding black, & everything wears a neater appearance.

We were heartily cheered along our route. Arriving at Seymour about 1.30 PM. Changed cars & took the Ohio & Miss RRd.

The citizens particularly the ladies are very friendly, doing all in their power to make us comfortable.

Left Seymour at 8 P.M. running rapidly. A few miles out of town the train stopped to water. Several ladies came with water & cake, speaking very kindly in cheering us on our way.

Left our little pet dog which we brought from Danville Ky, with them to remember us by.

Tuesday, June 9, 1863.

Aroused at 5 AM. After a restless night, by this time we had reached Vincennes, Ind. 105 miles. Where we stopped for breakfast, receiving soft bread and coffee, plenty of butter to be had at 15¢! The town is beautifully located on level prairie land. The buildings are all substantial and neat, built detached from each other. Leaving Vincennes we crossed the Wabash & entered Illinois were heavily greeted everywhere, ladies flocking to the Railway stations bringing us food, flowers, & kind wishes.

Olney, Clay City & Centralia welcomed us warmly. The road was very straight running over prairie where as far as the eye could reach nothing but level ground to be seen.

Had pleasant chats with a number of pretty ladies exchanging cards & promises to write. At Centralia we were detained from 6 PM until nearly 11 & found it very agreeable.

Passed another uncomfortable night amongst the baggage, hot & close.

Wednesday, June 10, 1863.

Aroused about 8 AM at Cairo, found it had been raining for some hours.

After considerable delay we were loaded on the Sallie Lisk and were considerably crowded for room. Cairo is a wretchedly dirty place presenting little to attract the stranger. Being recently paid & somewhat flush of money our boys made numerous purchases.

It was late in the afternoon before we left Cairo. Steaming down the Ohio we soon entered the Mississippi, and about sunset docked at Columbus Ky, for orders having been brought to by a shot across the bows. Columbus is well fortified, the old works occupied by the Rebs can be distinctly seen from the boat.

Leaving this place we ran on down until dark, when we again landed on the Kentucky shore & tied up for the night.

Slept very comfortably on the cabin floor.

During the afternoon and evening there was a great deal of rain; making everything very dirty.

Thursday, June 11, 1863.

Boat underweigh about 5 AM in a few hours passed the famous Island No 10,[71] where we touched for a few minutes

---

[71] Site of the Battle of Island Number Ten at the Kentucky Bend of the Mississippi River on February 28-April 8, 1862, the battle was an important Union victory.

from the boat little trace of the fight which occurred here could be seen.

The banks of the river are flat, heavily wooded & on account of the continued sameness, very uninteresting. I am greatly disappointed in the general appearance & size of the Mississippi.

After a comparatively uninteresting run we arrived at Memphis Ten shortly after 9 PM. Where we overtook a fleet of boats with other portions of our Corps.

Wrote to SR. G—.

Friday, June 12, 1863.

Opens clear and very warm a large fleet of transports for Vicksburg left early this morning.

Ventured on shore and took a short stroll, but the uncertainty of our stay makes all cautious.

Memphis presents evidence of once enjoying a large trade, there are scores of large buildings lying empty, and many others, hotels & business block used as hospitals.

The trade of the place at present is almost entirely in the hands of Jews, who make us pay roundly for everything.

Near our boat there are two of the iron clad monitor boats with mortars, used at Island No 10, also numerous captured guns, some of which are heavy pieces.

Night finds still at Memphis.

Saturday, June 13, 1863.

Clear and hot.

Vacated the boat in order to have it policed, the regiment repaired to Court Square to remain in the shade. Stacked arms and wandered at will. Quite a relief to get off the hot & crowded boat. Was up & down through the city eating ice cream & drinking soda water.

Having $10.50 in gold remaining I disposed of it at 40% premium. Several boats arrived from Vicksburg bringing wounded, cotton & prisoners.

Sunday, June 14, 1863.

Clear and hot.

Again off the boat and to Court Square, remaining there all day, lounging in the shade. All the transports except our own pulled out and went down stream this afternoon.

Attended Presbyterian Church in the evening.

Monday, June 15, 1863.

Another hot and clear day and again the regiment goes to Court Square.

The Provost troops here are becoming jealous saying we are to supersede them, a most absurd notion. Wrote to S.AM and sent E.T.M—. a copy of the "Memphis Bulletin."

Finished Dickens Dombey and Son.

Tuesday, June 16, 1863.

Still clear and hot.

In the morning Sam G [and] I visited Fort Pickering on the bluffs below the city.

The fortification is extensive one portion being garrisoned by Darkey troops, who commenced doing duty today.

Purchased and commenced reading David Copperfield.[72]

Heavy thunder shower in afternoon.

Wrote to SW Kipe in ev'g.

The night was cool and pleasant.

Wednesday, June 17, 1863.

Clear but cool and pleasant.

Left our landing at Memphis about 7 A.M. and pulled down the river, growing hot and sultry towards noon.

Touched at Helena Arkansas for orders, this post is strongly fortified & garrisoned, it's natural advantages are great.

In the stream laying at anchor was a U.S. Gunboat formerly the rebel boat Genl Bragg. Genl Prentiss the Commandant of the post was on the wharf boat.

Shortly after 4 P.M. Lieut Fox of the 27th Mich, died on board of Congestive fever had been unconscious four hours. Had a heavy storm accompanied with rain in the afternoon.

Tied up on the Arkansas shore, below the mouth of White river, at 8.30 P.M.

Thursday, June 18, 1863.

Under way early but moving very slowly, as we are under convoy of a U.S. Gunboat which has also a number of

---

[72] *David Copperfield* (1850) by Charles Dickens

85

heavily loaded tows in charge. We are going but little faster than the current of the streams. Wrote to Miss Minerva Scott, Centralia Ills. At 11 A.M. we were as Gaines landing, and at 1 P.M. our Gunboat escort left us. Through the Southern part of Arkansas signs of cultivation became plain, immense levees protecting large plantations could be distinctly seen, large plantation houses surrounded by their darkey quarters become numerous.

Tied up for the night at the mouth of Lake Providence canal. Went ashore in Louisiana and visited Genl W—. on board steamer Emperor. Across country we are 30 miles from Vicksburg. Heavy firing was heard in that direction yesterday, all quiet today.

Friday, June 19, 1863.

Opens beautifully clear, and cool. Arrived at Young's point opposite the mouth of Yazoo, at 9 A.M. 10 miles by water and 7 by land from Vicksburg.

Under way again at 11 AM heading up the Yazoo, touched at Chickasaw Bluffs and arriving at about 1 P.M, Snyder's Bluff which was recently captured from the Rebs, who had it strongly intrenched. The afternoon was excessively hot and close, went into camp about 4 miles from the landing, on high ground, so much broken that scarce a level spot was to be found.

Here we rejoined our brigade. Water is exceedingly scarce, ripe blackberries abundant.

Slept under a tree, turning in very tired.

Our regiment and private baggage came up in rather a damaged state many things missing. Supposed to have been stolen by deck hands on boat.

Saturday, June 20, 1863.

Awakened before day by the sound of heavy cannonading which proved to be the bombardment of Vicksburg, this continued until 9 A.M then ceased and was resumed in the evening. Some of the reports were exceedingly heavy.

Was busy all day repairing damage sustained by our Hospital Stores some of the boxes were much broken, and required repacking.

Sunday, June 21, 1863.

Clear and hot.

Not so much firing a[s] yesterday, lay quietly in the shade.

Mail in the evening but no letters for me.

We have strange and startling [news] from Penna. Rebel invasion and a general calling out of troops.[73]

Monday, June 22, 1863.

Clear and hot.

Black berrying in morning had a fine mess.

Marching orders in afternoon moved about 3 PM. Going about 4 miles and encamped in a cotton field, very rough

---

[73] In response to Army of Northern Virginia's invasion of Pennsylvania in June 1863, Governor Andrew Curtin called for 50,000 volunteers to take up arms in the volunteer militia.

ground, and water 1 ½ miles away. 150 of our men at work on a new line of entrenchments to protect our rear.

Tuesday, June 23, 1863.

Hot as usual with storm of wind and rain in evening.

Nothing of importance occurred today.

Wednesday, June 24, 1863.

Cloudy but sultry.

Established hospital and have one patient.—Carl Presit[74] Co 'G.'

The firing at Vicksburg has been unusually heavy throughout the day, and continues at night. Warren McHenry Asst Sug'n 6th Missouri and Nath Wike of 8th Missouri, now lying at Vicksburg, visited us today, they are both old Columbians.

My diet now is about one half blackberries, which I pick about 5 minutes walk from camp.

We have a rumor today of 'Port Hudson'[75] having surrendered at 4 PM. Yesterday.

Thursday, June 25, 1863.

Opens clear and hot.

---

[74] Private Carl Presit was recruited from Tioga County and mustered into service on September 29, 1861. Wounded at the Battle of Spotsylvania Court House, Virginia on May 14, 1864 he was later transferred to the Veterans Reserve Corps on May 4, 1865.

[75] The Siege of Port Hudson, Louisiana ended on July 9, 1863, when Confederate Major General Franklin Kitchell Gardner (1823-1873) surrendered his forces to Union Major General Nathanial P. Banks (1816-1894).

The firing at Vicksburg continues, it seems to have become a settled thing now and is but little remarked on. Our sick list is pretty heavy, mostly diarrhea cases, another man admitted to Hosptl. In the afternoon the noise of a severe engagement at Vicksburg reached us. In the evening the light shells and cannonading could be distinctly seen.

Friday, June 26, 1863.

Clear and hot.

Was busily employed all day, rearranging things generally. The firing today is not so heavy, only an occasional gun is heard.

The dull routine of camp is again upon us.

Saturday, June 27, 1863.

As usual hot, the heat seems to be increasing.

Heavy details from our regiment still continues at work on the entrenchments.

News from the front are cheering.

S.B.G and self went blackberrying in afternoon gathered about 6 qrts—.

Under orders to be ready to march at a moments notice, with 5 days rations on hand.

Sunday, June 28, 1863.

The great heat continues, a little breeze occasionally is all that relieves us. Water is distant and soon becomes warm.

Two more men admitted to Hosptl, Geo Backus[76] Co G, and Charles Johnson,[77] Co A. SB Clipper of Co B. detailed for an additional attendant. Very little firing at Vicksburg, on the whole it has been a very quiet day.

Monday, June 29, 1863.

Still clear and hot.

Our Division, moved this morning, going about six miles, the sick in hosptl and Quarters, were left behind.

I remaining in charge of Hosptl &c. Capt. Curtin in charge of the camp and men in quarters.

After the troops passed on all went quietly as usual.

Geo. Seitz[78] of Co 'K.' admitted to hospital this evening. Seriously ill with Dysentery.

In the absence of the brigade medical authorities, I signed the commissary's abstract for May, brought in today showing a new balance of $114.—. in our favor.

This much in five months. The nights are beautifully clear and moonlight but mosquitoes & gnats make it impossible to sleep until after midnight.

---

[76] Private George H. Backus was recruited from Tiago County and mustered into service on September 18, 1861.

[77] Private Charles Johnson was recruited from Centre County and mustered into service on August 16, 1861. Johnson was killed at Petersburg, Virginia on July 30, 1864.

[78] Private John G. Seitz was recruited from Lancaster County and mustered into service on March 27, 1862.

Tuesday, June 30, 1863.

The weather as yesterday, or if any change it grows hotter. Dr Tyler, 1 Asst Surg. Of 36 Mass, attended our sick. Had a busy time this morning, the men in Hosptl are improving.

The air is so dry and hot that the least exertion produces copious perspiration.

At the order of the 3rd Division sent a large box of bandages for Brig Supplies to the Division, they seem to anticipate a fight.

One half of 1863 is gone, and still the war continues. Another beautiful moonlight night by the light of the moon I finished David Copperfield.

The heavy guns at Vicksburg are playing and their heavy booming breaks loudly on the quiet night.

Still no letters from home.

Wednesday, July 1, 1863.

As usual dry and hot.

The firing on the front is quite brisk this morning.

No surgeon in attendance today for cause or other. So have to shift best way I can. Recd a few supplies from Sanitary Commission. In the evening Dr Youndt brought two more hospl patients. R. Roberts drummer Co 'K.' right fore arm broken, and James Malligan,[79] Co 'A' helpless with Rheumatism. So we are full up, as I had admitted Wm Utter[80]

---

[79] Private James Malligan was recruited from Centre County and mustered into service on August 16, 1861. On October 11, 1863, Malligan was transferred into the Veteran Reserve Corps.

of Co H. earlier in the evening. The mail to-day brought me letters from S.A.M., S.R.G., E.G.T., and M.E.H. the first mail I have received since 6th ult. Wrote to Bro ETM.

Made inventory of med supplies on hand.

Thursday, July 2, 1863.

Clear and hot, everything is becoming dry and parched, those intolerable pests mosquitoes prevent sleep at night and the flies in daytime. A few weeks of such weather and exposure & our regiment will be small, it is very exhausting.

The firing on the front was kept up through the night by the heavy guns & this morning they are firing rapidly.

Dr. Maxwell returned to Camp and assumed charge of Hospl. Rigged up a mosquito bar today and have a promise of a good night's rest.

Friday, July 3, 1863.

Over cast, but very sultry.

The cannonading at Vicksburg has the night & this morning been very rapid & heavy. Made inventory of Brig supplies and sent to Dr Christ.

About 5 P.M. the cannonading ceased and all remained quiet through the night. Had a slight shower of rain about 9.30 PM.

Saturday, July 4, 1863.

---

[80] Private William Utter was recruited from Tioga County and mustered into service on September 18, 1861. Captured by the Confederates, Utter was moved to the prisoner of war camp at Andersonville, Georgia where he died on November 23, 1864.

The national birthday.

Opens rather quietly, a few heavy guns, in the direction of Vicksburg sounding more like salutes than otherwise.

Early in the morning rumors that Vicksburg had surrendered were flying around, but it was not until afternoon that the glorious news was confirmed.

It surrendered at 5 AM. Giving into our hands many thousands of prisoners & a large number of guns &c. Surely a fitting cause for rejoicing and remembering the day. In afternoon heard that our division was on the move, going after Johnston.[81] A number of sick from the regiment were sent back and we must remain.

Dr. Maxwell and I spent the evening at a farm house near by. On the whole the day has passed quietly, but the fall of Vicksburg has crowned it gloriously.

Sunday, July 5, 1863.

The weather seems to grow hotter. Another ambulance load of sick came back from the regiment, bringing us a large mail, letters from S.A.M., L.S.J., S.R.G., C.E.G., M.M.S. & N.W., the two letters from Centralia Ills, beside 6 newspapers, dating from May 30th to June 25th.

In all we have about 40 sick men in hospital & camp.

The whole care of the division sick has been placed on Dr Maxwell who has been busily engaged carrying out his orders.

---

[81] General Joseph E. Johnston (1807-1891), commander of the Army of the Tennessee.

Among the latter to concentrate the hospitals, & tomorrow we are to move to near the Milldale church on the Bluff.

There is much trouble obtaining transportation, teams & ambulances being all employed.

Monday, July 6, 1863.

After awaiting all morning for teams to move, and none were arriving the orders to move were countermanded. In the afternoon accompanied Dr M—. in visiting the Hospls of the 17th & 27th Mich & of the 3rd Brig also to make arrangements to draw rations for our men, from the commissary boat, this was attended with much trouble, but was finally arranged with Genl C.C. Washburne Commanding the Post, who treated us very civilly.

A storm of rain with thunder overtook us towards evening. The Hospl that of the 79th NY was visited after 9 P.M. The night was [dark] and while returning our ambulance was upset and Dr. M was seriously injured, three ribs were broken and he was otherwise bruised by moving carefully succeeded in getting the Dr back to camp and attended to, he suffered severely. In the upset I made my escape by jumping from the ambulance.

There is much suffering in the regimental hospitals, medical attendance & medicine was being sadly needed, and the locations of many are very bad.

Wrote to S.A.M.

Tuesday, July 7, 1863.

Hot again. Dr. Maxwell is fast abed. Q.M. Sergt Mullins arrived bringing us quit a mail for me a letter from Bro

E.T.M & several papers. In afternoon got the chaplains horse and went after rations, first to secure transportation, in this Q.M. Sergt aided me, then to Genl Washburne to have requisitions approved & then to the commissary. Thus occupied until nearly night, returned to camp with the rations, where I arrived about 9 P.M. heartily tired. Shortly after this had a heavy storm of rain thunder and lighting, which continued through the night.

Drew rations for 55 men. Turned in feeling quite unwell & much fatigued, having ridden about 10 miles.

Wednesday, July 8, 1863.

The day opens sultry, though the rain of the past night settled the dust, which makes it altogether pleasant.

Issued the rations to the men, and passed a somewhat busy day.

Dr M. is improving slowly.

Thursday, July 9, 1863.

Hot and clear.
Sick list coming down rapidly nearly all are convalesant. Beginning to feel better but have numerous little ulcers in my mouth, which are exceedingly painful.
Wrote to Sallie R.G—. Spent the evening pleasantly at Mr Hall's.

Friday, July 10, 1863.

Hot and clear.

Sick list still coming down, and I am more at leisure, which is welcome in this hot climate.

Wrote to M.E.H & M.M.S. Time drags slowly on, rumors of a move northward continue but we have nothing tangible. By Cincinnati papers of 3rd inst. We have exciting news of doings in Pennsylvania.[82]

Saturday, July 11, 1863.

Opens as usually.

A heavy rain at noon accompanied by thunder & lighting. Had another trip to Genl Washburne's & the commissary boat, after rations, only a part of which could be brought up.

Monday, July 20, 1863.

Since July 11th all has gone on monotonously, an occasional rain storm, but the weather mostly hot, the past few days have been excessively warm. Every 5 days I have had the ration job over again attended with more or less difficulty. Numerous rumors & reports reach us from the front, but nothing can be positively ascertained from our Brigade.

The news from Penna have been cheering. We have daily expected orders to move northward again, but they are still delayed. The sick have been doing well, thus far no deaths, although we have had two severe cases. Have had

---

[82] The Battle of Gettysburg, Pennsylvania was fought on July 1-3, 1863 was a significant Union victory.

considerable riding to do, & am becoming quite accustomed to the saddle.

Tuesday, July 21, 1863.

Clouded but warm.

Flies and mosquitoes are very troublesome.

From good authority we have it that our Corps is now on its return march & may be looked for hourly.

An intensely hot day.

Wednesday, July 22, 1863.

Clear and hot, the advance of our Corps is beginning to come in.[83] About 4 P.M. Dr Christ arrived with 3 wounded and a large number of sick men. Soon our had our hands full getting them under shelter & feeding.

Among the wounded was my intimate friend Sam G—. shot in the leg, a severe but not dangerous wound, which he bears most cheerfully. Aside of him is Sergt Carvey[84] of Co. I also

---

[83] The Siege of Vicksburg, Mississippi ended on July 4, 1863 with the surrender of Confederate Lieutenant General John C. Pemberton's (1814-1881) Army of Vicksburg to Union Major General Ulysses S. Grant's (1822-1885) Army of the Tennessee. Following the Siege of Vicksburg, the IX Corps was moved to the Siege of Jackson, Mississippi, where Union Major General William T. Sherman (1820-1891) forces surrounded the city on July 10, 1863. The siege ended on July 13, 1863, when Confederate forces led by General Joseph E. Johnston evacuated the city.

[84] 1st Sergeant Edwin B. Carvey was recruited from Tiago County and mustered into service on September 21, 1861. Promoted to Sergeant on July 1, 1863, Carvey was wounded at Jackson, Mississippi on July 11, 1863. After his recovery, Carvey was transferred to the Veterans Reserve Corps on November 18, 1863 where he remained until the expiration of his term of service and was mustered out on October 20, 1864.

wounded in the leg. The sick are mostly down with Int. Fever and exhaustion.

Lieut Humphreys[85] & Sergt Hill[86] of Co F. were killed also Corpl Noble of I. All excellent men. Private Divald[87] of F died on the return from disease, those who were wounded were hurt at Jackson, on July 11th.

A shower of rain about 5 PM.

Thursday, July 23, 1863.

Opens clear and hot.

The boys all feel better for their night's rest and nourishing food, and seem bright this morning. About noon the regiment returned to camp, heartily glad to be back again. The men all show marks of hardships through which they have gone. Severe marching with little else than green corm & green fruit, to eat for several days. All are dirty and [illegible] but have done most excellent service. Soap, water & plenty to eat will bring them out nicely. Heard for the first time of the burning of the Columbia Bridge & the close proximity of the Rebs to the folks at home. Had a slight rain in afternoon.

A large proportion of Co K is sick with fever & ague.

Recd a letter from Sallie R. G—. also a number Presses'.

---

[85] 2nd Lieutenant Richard Humphrey was recruited from Wayne or Tiago County and mustered into service on October 1, 1861. Promoted from 1st Sergeant, Humphrey was killed at Jackson, Mississippi on July 11, 1863.

[86] Sergeant Lewis P. F. Hill was recruited from Wayne or Tiago County and mustered into service on September 8, 1861. Hill was killed at Jackson, Mississippi on July 11, 1863.

[87] Private Civilian Divald was recruited from Wayne or Tiago County and mustered into service on October 8, 1861. Divald died on July 22, 1863.

Friday, July 24, 1863.

Clear & hot.

Busy all day. Taken sick in afternoon with violent headache and fever, and by evening was fast abed, with bilious fever promising fair to hold me for sometime.

Saturday, July 25, 1863.

Still abed, fever abating but pains in head, limbs and back very severe.

A few sick come scattering in still.

Sunday, July 26, 1863.

Abed yet but growing better commenced on Quinine in afternoon & am improving.

Pain in back very severe but head less so.

Monday, July 27, 1863.

Still keep my bed, and continue on Quinine, in consequence of having taken morphine last night this day occurrences are very indistinct.

Tuesday, July 28, 1863.

Much better, but do not attempt to do much yet. Moved around a little.

Had a tremendous storm of rain thunder and lightning this afternoon.

No news of the boats yet. All anxious to leave

Wednesday, July 29, 1863.

Up and at work again feeling weak an unsteady with a not altogether clear head. Yet pushed along and made out a busy day.

Geo Seitz of Co K died this 9 AM and old man and long sick, buried in afternoon.

The rest of sick are generally doing well. We have had at times as many as 44 in hospl, today we have 40, & excused sick in quarters 15, an unusual number for 45th.

Recd letter from Bro E.T.M. dated 16th, giving me the [illegible] news that all had passed safely through their recent severe trials. Commenced a letter to Parents.

Thursday, July 30, 1863.

Opens bright and clear, with a fine cool breeze blowing.

Sick all improving, and as we are under marching orders, had a general pack up of medicines, marking boxes & making preparations for our journey northward. Withal I had a very busy day.

In the evening received orders to have the sick ready to move in morning & they go on a separate boat and will be accompanied by cooks and nurse, there will be about 34 sent which will give us quite a time of rest again.

A pleasant moonlight night.

Friday, July 31, 1863.

Opens cool and overcast, but proved a warm day. Settled up with the Commissary for the month.

A long day constantly awaiting the orders to move the sick but none arrived.

Late in afternoon Jacob Hendershott,[88] private of Co A died very suddenly in quarters, had been complaining of Chill & Fever, and not thought very sick, though it may have been a [illegible] chill, a number of similar cases have occurred recently in other regiments.

Exchanged my old "Antietam [illegible]" for a wooden one obtained of a Rebel at Vicksburg. Received by mail 2 [illegible] mailed on 16th.

Saturday, August 1, 1863.

Opens clear and bright, but warm. Attended the funeral of D. Hendershott immediately after sunrise, it was done in true military style.

Geo H. Backus, private, of Co 'G' died in Hospital at 11.30 AM, his disease was diarrhea, he had been sick a long time. A large mail was received, brought me a letter from S.R.G—. and two papers.

Had a heavy storm of rain accompanied by thunder and lightning, lasting for about an hour in the afternoon, which cooled the atmosphere finally.

Geo Backus was buried at sundown.

The long looked for final order to move the sick came just at supper time, they were all taken away in one train of ambulances. Sent four nurses and two cooks along, this looks like move in earnest and we may now hope that a few

---

[88] Private David Hendershott was recruited from Centre County and mustered into service on August 16, 1861.

days more will end our stay in Mississippi. All is quiet and lonely around the hospital to-night—.

Sunday, August 2, 1863.

Clear and bright.

The Sick Call passed off rapidly though there were quite a number in attendance. Wrote to Bro E.T.M.—. About noon four of the men whom we sent off last evening were returned, & report not sufficient room & poor accommodations. It is too bad that after so much delay, insufficient preparations should been made, surely the men who have endured this Campaign deserve all the attention that could be given them. There seems some fatal neglect somewhere, which I trust may be severely punished.

Another shower in afternoon but not so heavy as yesterday, serving to cool the air somewhat.

Great difficulty has been had with the rations for some days past. All day today the men have been without hard bread, a supply arrived this evening.

Attended divine service by our Chaplin this evening, the first in this State.

Monday, August 3, 1863.

Clear and bright.

A quiet but hot day. News to-night that we are to leave tomorrow at 8 AM. It seems almost too good to be true.

Tuesday, August 4, 1863.

Clear, bright and intensely hot.

Up early and packed up ready to move. The regiment left Camp at 9 AM. I followed at about 10 AM, arriving at the landing found no boat for us, so sat around anxiously waiting for the boat until dark, none coming turned in among mosquitoes &c, on the bank of the Yahoo. Awakened about 11.30 PM, by the arrival of a large boat the Hiawatha, up and ready to load but no orders, turned in again about 3 AM, and slept soundly until daylight.

The night was beautiful moonlight, but mosquitoes intolerable—.

Wednesday, August 5, 1863.

Opens clear and warm.

Up at daylight and to work stowing baggage, hot job in the hold. After some difficulty got all snuggly fixed, & self with medicine in the forward cabin. The boat is a large and handsome side wheeler, recently fitted up.

We have on board Benjamin's Battery, of 20 pds Parrott's, 36th Mass, 27th Mich, our own regiment and a number of teams with mules & horses almost without number, crowding on boat most uncomfortably.

The men finally loaded and pulled out about 5 PM. Down the Yazoo to Mississippi and then down until within sight of Vicksburg, where we met the Express & took on board forage for the teams, about ship & we are heading for the north & the land of good water.

Had a slice of a Mississippi melon, first of season, price $1.00 each for moderate size ones. Bid Genl Welsh good bye on Yazoo landing, looking very well.

Thursday, August 6, 1863.

Cloudy and pleasant.

Had a very comfortable night on the cabin floor.

Touched at Lake Providence La. Early in the morning.

Running very slowly and making but poor time. Spent a half hour at sunset on the hurricane deck, enjoying the cool of the evening, and having a pleasant chat with Capt Belger of the 8th Mich now on the staff of

Friday, August 7, 1863.

Over cast and where any air stirring, cool and pleasant, but the cabin is hot and close. Early in the morning we were off the mouth of White river, slowly working up stream.

At 7 PM we touched at Helena Arkansas, remaining but a few minutes.

A much larger number of troops are lying here now then when we went down.

Saturday, August 8, 1863.

Opens bright and warm.

The sick list continues quite heavy. Int Fever and diarrhea are the principal diseases.

By 10 AM we were at Memphis, went ashore and found things much as we had left them when coming down. Had a run around town with Dr. Youndt in search of a few medical supplies, which we seceded finally in obtaining.

It is now 1 PM & I sitting in the old court square.

The troops were debarked at the coal landing & enjoyed the day on shore but were not allowed the freedom of town.

Left Memphis about 5.30 PM.

Sunday, August 9, 1863.

Bright clear and quiet.

Hard at work all morning having my own sick & those of Benjamin's Battery to supply. A private of 36th Mass died on board.

Formed quite a pleasant acquaintance with a gentleman from Ypsilanti Mich. A brother Chip. Samson by name.

In the evening made out requisitions for medical supplies for the quarter.

Touched at Island No 10 late in the evening.

Wrote to S.R.G—.

Monday, August 10, 1863.

Clear and bright.

Arrived at Cairo between 8 & 9 AM. And by evening had all my traps safely stowed on board the cars. The 36th Mass. Left before dark. We are bound for Cincinnati.

Sent all sick except a few slight cases by boat to Cincinnati.

A mail arrived today but no news for me.

Had a severe fall down stairs on boat this morning bruising my back.

Tuesday, August 11, 1863.

Opens clouded and cool.

Did not get asleep until about 2.30 AM when we left Cairo, aroused at 6 AM at Jonesboro.

A pleasant run up through the country. Near Irvington the body of one of the 36th Mass was found, life was extinct, he had evidently fallen off during the night, was taken on the train to Centralia and left for burial. Stopped at Centralia for dinner. At 2 PM we arrived at Sandoval.

Which place we left about Sundown passing a few towns before dark.

Wednesday, August 12, 1863.

After a restless night opens on us at Washington Indiana. About 2 AM we stopped at Vincennes for Coffee & Bread.

At Seymour we stopped a long while and had coffee, melons & fruit are very plenty and we are making free use of them.

Towards evening we stopped at Lorcoran & large and important place on the RRd, there being a large depot & car works here, leaving here we soon arrived at Lawrenceburg, another quite large place. At both of these we were heartily cheered & welcomed by the ladies.

Shortly after leaving Lawrenceburg we crossed the [illegible] and entered Ohio, and about 10 PM arrived at Cincinnati & disembarked the Regt going to the Refreshment Salon & thence to Covington, & I remaining at the depot with the baggage, where I passed a tolerably comfortable night.

Thursday, August 13, 1863.

Opens pleasant. After brushing up a little, started out in search of breakfast and to see something of the town, took breakfast at the Washington Saloon and had a good meal. Returning to the Depot, assisted in loading up the baggage, which was done in the roughest manner. Went up town again, made a number of purchases of little necessities. Near the Burnett House met with Saml Wright of Columbia recently appointed on Genl Welsh's staff, he brought several letters date July 6th. Visited Peurt Erwin & Harry Martin the latter in Adam's Express office.

Learned from a private telegram that Genl W—. was sick and would arrive that night.

Crossed to Covington Ky and found the baggage at the Depot, & the troop in camp beyond the city. In comp'y with Corpl Snyder visited Cincinnati in search of Sam G who had arrived the day previous. Went to West End Hospl but could get no trace of him. After seeing a good portion of city returned & finding the baggage ordered out to camp, also went there & established myself.

One year in Service today.

Friday, August 14, 1863.

Bright and pleasant. Settling down to Camp life again, our camp is quite a pleasant one on a large common beyond the city. Huckster women are bringing in quantities of provisions of all kinds. Our sick list is large. Diarrhea the principal complaint.

Established a hospital and patients are coming in.

Remained in camp all day. In evening took a short stroll into Covington.

In the evening we received the sad news that our noble Genl Welsh had died in Cincinnati a few hours before of Congestive chill. It is so sudden and unlooked for that we [illegible] can realize our loss. He was a friend to us all and each will deeply feel his loss.

The body is to be sent home tomorrow, what a blow will it be for our little town, & that family he loved so well.

Paymaster has left the pay rolls & will commence paying tomorrow.

Saturday, August 15, 1863.

Clear and bright.

Sick call very large, some seven cases of diarrhea.

J. Brenneman & I visited Cincinnati and found Sam G— in the Washington Park Hospl doing very well and in good spirits. Also found a number of our sick boys in same Hospital, doing well.

Met Matth Cowden who was over the city with us.

Have been making free use of Ice Cream & peaches & c. which are very abundant.

Returned to Camp in afternoon after having had a pleasant trip.

Paymaster arrived & commenced paying off; paid 4 companies by dark, and then stopped. Feel quite unwell, & take a dose of [illegible].

Sunday, August 16, 1863.

Sick list continues large.

Kept as quiet as possible all morning as I fell very lowly. In afternoon had a very pleasant visit from Wm H— Garrigus Sams brother of Salem Ohio, who remained until evening, taking a view of soldiers life which is all new to him.

At Dress Parade this evening an order from Col Morrison[89] Commdg Brigade, relative to the death of Genl Welsh was read.

Had a fine shower this afternoon. Late at night received orders to be ready to march at 6 AM tomorrow.

Monday, August 17, 1863.

Bright and clear.

Up early and packed up ready to move, left camp shortly after 7 AM, and took the baggage to the K.C RRd depot where we waited until afternoon before we loaded made a short trip to Cincinnati and bought me a new haversack, ($3.00) where I again met WHG—.

Finally about 3 PM started on the rail. Our car was attached to a regular passenger train & moved rapidly, about sundown reached Paris our camping ground of April last, our old seemed pleased to see us again. On to Lexington and then to Nicholasville.

Slept in the car as we did not unload, and passed quite a comfortable night although I had a high fever in afternoon.

---

[89] Colonel William Ralls Morrison (1824-1909) 17th Illinois Volunteer Infantry Regiment.

Tuesday, August 18, 1863.

Slept late and found a cool and pleasant morning feeling somewhat better than last night. The Regt arrived & immediately started for Camp some three miles from town. Having but one wagon it took all day to send out the baggage and I did not arrive in camp until evening, where I found the paymaster hard at work & received my pay to July 1st.

Left 25 sick men in Nicholasville unable to march to camp.

It was dark before had quarters arranged and turned in fatigued.

Wednesday, August 19, 1863.

Clear and warm with a pleasant wind in afternoon. Put up Hospital and started with two patients with a fair prospect for an unlimited number more. In afternoon had a sharp chill followed with a high fever which kept me on my back all the balance of the day and night.

Mail at night, seven Presses, a letter from Home July 28th & one from Mrs L.S.J.

Thursday, August 20, 1863.

Clear and bright.

Feeling somewhat better and attended the Sick Call, which was very large. Scarcely able to see it through!

Hospital patients coming in to-night we have 13 patients on hand, those left at Nicholasville were brought up.

Friday, August 21, 1863.

Overcast partially with a little rain in afternoon.

Feeling exceedingly dull and languid, to use a common expression: "I'm played out," worn down with service, and today I feel very much inclined to apply for a short leave, as rest I must have and cannot get it here. Were Dr Christ with us I think I should apply.

Have a great deal to do. Sick Call occupied two full hours steady, and the stragglers the balance of the morning and much of the afternoon. By mail received a lot of papers and a letter from SRG & one from SAM. Rumor says we are to prepare for the field again, which seems in the present condition of the corps to be ridiculous.

Wrote to SBG- & sent him his mail.

Saturday, August 22, 1863.

Clear & warm.

Feeling somewhat better. Another busy morning.

Gen Fourenu has arrived he is to command our Division, has been riding around the camp.

Tuesday, August 25, 1863.

A cold wet day, heavy rain in morning.

Woolen underclothing feeling exceedingly comfortable.

Dr C— arrived at noon, had been in Illinois. Part of our medicine arrived. Dr. Youndt, left for Cin' Ohio for Sanitary Stores. Our sick list continues exceedingly heavy, for several days past have been very unwell myself. At times unable to do any duty—but most of the time dragging along. Yesterday was a very poor day, but today goes better. Had a very busy afternoon.

Wednesday, August 26, 1863.

Partially overcast with rough cold winds, rumors of moving flying through camp, and night brought the order to move at daylight tomorrow. All sick left back, and I must be again behind. Am considerably out of humor about it, I seem unfortunate in this respect.

A partial division of medicines was made & retain some with the chest.

Thursday, August 27, 1863.

Clear and bright, up at daylight and finished packing up the medicine for move. The Brigade moved off promptly, the 79th N.Y. on the night the regiment were small leaving many sick behind. I am left with more than a hundred sick men, a few medicines and many promises of supplies and medical attendance, which promises I'm afraid are too glowing.

At noon found Cyrus Mann[90] of Co H growing worse, after much trouble obtained a Surgeon to see who proscribed and left. At 10 minutes past 4 PM he died, disease—Congestive Chill—

Have enough on hand to worry both and body. Wrote to SRG—. & a short letter to WHM—

After waiting no Surgeon arrived to attend to our men.

---

[90] Private Cyrus Mann was recruited from Tiago County and mustered into service on September 18, 1861.

Friday, August 28, 1863.

Clouded with showers of rain. Much rain in afternoon. Dr Smith of 27th Mich. Attended Sick Call, there seems some improvement in the general condition of the men.

The old stand by Quinine gone out today and when a new supply will come from cannot be seem.

Wrote to E.T.M.

Saturday, August 29, 1863.

Clear and bright, but a strong chilly wind blowing steadily.

Drew rations for my men to-day and found on footing up that I had 148 to ration. Issued the rations to each company myself which gave me quite a full job. The sick with one or two exceptions are improving. We obtained straw for our Hospital bunks today which makes them more comfortable. Jno Campbell[91] of Co F. died at 7.45 this evening, he had been sinking in a typhoid state for several days.

Sunday, August 30, 1863.

Clear and bright but opens quite cold, the past night has been a cold one with frost. Dr. Youndt arrived from Cincinnati, and as he has be ordered to remain here it removes much from my mind.

Still no medical supplies, although much in need yet some of our neighbors are faring far worse. Have had quite a busy day yet my health is so much better that I do not mind it now. Capt Lewis Martin[92] of Co K. returned from Genl Hospl has

---

[91] Private John Campbell was recruited from Wayne or Tioga County and mustered into service on September 3, 1861.

[92] Corporal Lewis Martin was recruited from Lancaster County and

been to Columbia and brought me shirts & c also a letter of late date.

Monday, August 31, 1863.

Clear, bright and pleasant, the morning and evening not so cool. Still plenty to do. Orders and counter orders in plenty. Ordered to prepare a list of men to be sent to regiment to-morrow, so have made a list of 50 and rationed them for 3 days.

Tuesday, September 1, 1863.

The first day of Autumn opens bright and pleasant.

Only a portion of the men ordered forward to the Regt were sent off this morning leaving me about 100 men on hand.

By mail received letter of Aug 19th from Bro Will.

Wednesday, September 2, 1863.

A pleasant day. Wrote to Bro Will. Still kept tolerably busy between the dispensing of medicine and the Commissary. Have 107 men including myself on hand. Geo Moyer[93] of Co "C" died at 7.20 PM. Disease Diphtheria, the first case in our Hospital, he was seemingly doing very well in the morning, but a change for the worse took place in afternoon. Division head quarters moved to the front to day.

Thursday, September 3, 1863.

Cloudy with a little rain.

---

mustered into service on August 22, 1861. Martin died in 1864 at Louisville, Kentucky.

[93] Private George N. Moyer was recruited from Mifflin County and mustered into service on September 19, 1861.

Geo Moyer was buried this morning, had a firing party and drums of our own, the funeral was well conducted.

Things are going quietly in the camp.

Friday, September 4, 1863.

Received letters from S.R.G. and S.B.G—. had been to Crab Orchard and sent back.

Orders this evening for shipping another lot of sick & convalescents to-morrow.

Received this evening our Sanitary Supplies, rather late in the day for use here, they are not very satisfactory.

Saturday, September 5, 1863.

Opens clouded.

Sent forward a large portion of our men. Some in wagons & others on foot, leaving but a small party behind. In afternoon shipped 8 of our sickest men to Camp Nelsons Hospital leaving but 4 in Hospl who are to go tomorrow. Also sent Dr Christ two nurses.

Wrote to SRG, WHG & SRG.

Sunday, September 6, 1863.

Sent forward another small detachment including the sick officers. Present prospects indicate our speedy breaking up here. This has been my quietest day, a day of rest, little doing.

Monday, September 7, 1863.

Dr Youndt started for the regiment this morning.

Had quite a busy morning capping up rolls for Dr Beviere, Surg in change of Camp. In latter part of afternoon shipped the remainder of the 46th NY, and then had a busy evening preparing to leave in morning.

Had quite an enticing offer of our Asst Surgeon if I would leave my own and go into another regiment. A thing I would not do, and a position I would not accept, as I would not fill it to my own satisfaction and content my own mind.

Tuesday, September 8, 1863.

Up at daylight and had a busy time loading our remnant. Started for Crab Orchard about 7 A.M. rode in an ambulance. About 11 AM. Were at Camp Dick Rob our old camp of last April. Arrived at Lancaster Shore after 1 PM and took dinner. Then over a rough and dusty road to Crab Orchard which we arrived in time for supper.

By favor of Capt Trout[94] received my razor & several letters from home.

Wednesday, September 9, 1863.

A busy day, first arranging my camp fixings for a stay of some length and then in evening disarranging them for a march to-morrow.

---

[94] Captain John F. Trout was recruited from Lancaster County and mustered into service in Co. B on September 2, 1861. Promoted to 2nd Lieutenant on August 1, 1862 and was transferred to Co. H on August 1, 1862 where he was promoted to Captain on January 15, 1863.

Made a general overhauling and repacking, rejecting and leaving behind many things as too cumbrous to carry, this kept me hard at work until after midnight, then turned in for a nap before the final break up.

Thursday, September 10, 1863.

Opens very foggy. After much bustle we are under way for Tennessee. Eight days rations besides ammunition and clothing are carried by the men, too much I am afraid for the long march ahead. The sick are left behind under charge of Dr Maxwell, luckily for me I'm not on that list now.

What remains of the old 45th start off briskly as though (and I believe it does) the same old spirit animates them, though they are now much worn by service. Twenty two, today and did not find it out until after starting. After a dusty march of 11 miles we halted for the night near Mt Vernon.

Scribbled a lead pencil note to Sister Sallie, and turned in quite tired.

Friday, September 11, 1863.

Reveille at 3 A.M. and march at 5 are the orders for today, as we are in rear of division do not get off until six. The country is hilly and roads becoming very rough. Today we passed over some exceedingly mountains country, the roads are the worst I have ever seen, in some places almost impassable for loaded wagons. Wagon wrecks are abundant along the entire route. Stopped after our noon rest & coffee besides a splendid pool of water among the mountains, about 4 PM crossed the Rock Castle river & continued our march until about 8 when we encamped on the bank of the Little Rock Castle, having marched about 17 miles, as the wagon did not come up slept without blankets & passed a tolerably comfortable night with no covering except a shelter tent.

Saturday, September 12, 1863.

Another early Reveille and daybreak march, in our first mile we encountered the highest and longest hill yet met. Still tugging up and down, with haversack growing lighter we reach and camp about 3 miles from London, between 9 & 10 AM. And received the welcome order, that we rest until Monday.

Wagon train still behind and in the evening had a heavy rain and had to pass a rather chilly and uncomfortable night with a gum blanket to lie on and nothing for cover.

Sunday, September 13, 1863.

Opens cloudy and damp.

We have fresh beef rations issued today, wagon arrived during the morning all safe and sound, replenished haversacks and had several good meals while cooking utensils were at hand.

Capt Diebler[95] of Co. 'B.' returned from furlough, bringing me a letter from Sister, and the information that Bro Will & A. Bruner were at Crab Orchard, to visit us, and would try to follow up, hope they may succeed.

---

[95] Captain John B. Diebler was recruited from Lancaster County and mustered into service on September 2, 1861. Promoted to 1st Sergeant on September 30, 1862, on March 1, 1863 Diebler was promoted to 1st Lieutenant. Diebler was promoted to Captain on July 1, 1864, and remained with the regiment until his resignation on October 20, 1864.

Our paymaster arrived this evening bringing our pay rolls, which we signed & expect to receive pay to-morrow when we camp.

Turn in with everything ready for an early move.

Monday, September 14, 1863.

Reveille at 3 & march at 5 AM.

Before sunrise we had passed through London and made 3 or four miles of new road.

The road is quite smooth & pleasant, the rain having laid the dust we march with much greater ease & by 1 PM had passed over 15 miles & went into camp.

On the way we met a body of 2550 rebel prisoners, recently taken at Cumberland Gap & on their way northward under guard, a most motley crew. Slung my knapsack again to-day to make sure of my blanket tonight.

One year ago today and I underwent my first experience in battle at South Mountain, how many who were comrades then have long since gone.

Tuesday, September 15, 1863.

Opens with a foggy morning with the reveille at 3 and march at 5 AM. This day we marched about 14 miles and came into camp beyond Bartoursville about noon. Camping besides the Cumberland whose waters I took a most excellent bath.

The last few hours of the march were very fatiguing owing to the intense heat, came into camp nearly used up. Wrote to SR.G. from whom I received a letter of 6th inst. This morning.

Wagon trains came in fine time.

Wednesday, September 16, 1863.

Foggy followed by a hot sun.

The old role of early start and marched 8 or 10 miles by about 10 AM. When we encamped near the Cumberland.

The pay master commenced paying about 6.30 PM.

Our road is quite pleasant but generally surrounded by knobs, with limited views of country, some of which is quite fine.

Received my pay to Sept 1st, $60.00. Added $15.00 and took an allotment draft No 84, Sept 16th, E. Van Volenburgh, for $75.—payable to my own order.

Thursday, September 17, 1863.

A warm quiet day in camp. The anniversary of the great Antietam fight of last year in which we took part.

We are to march again tomorrow at 6 AM. & to make short marches allowing the supply train to catch us.

Settled the August account with our Commissary and received $21.85, then settled with J. Urill and paying him $25.20 and Dr Youndt $1.60, money advanced for use of Hospl.

Friday, September 18, 1863.

Opens cloudy with rain, hard heavy rain during the night. Orders to march countermanded, and we are doing our best to be comfortable by our camp fires, drying our wet blankets and tents.

*Two of our attendants, Samuel Eyer[96] and David Bowen[97]
were returned to their companies by order of Col Hills. Dr
C- & he had considerable trouble about the matter. H-
seems not well inclined towards Hospital.*

Saturday, September 19, 1863.

*After a cold chilly night the morning opens cloudy. Reveille
at 4, and march at 6. Crossed Cumberland ford and camped
about 10 miles from the Gap.*

*Some of the scenery today among the knobs have been bold
& ragged, lofty peaks with rocky summits jutting
heavenward, & an occasional earthwork showing the foot
print of war. Crossed the Cumberland at the ford and
followed the view until at its junction with Straight Creek,
where we left it & crossed a mountain range. Camped for
the night on a pleasant flat surrounded on every side by
mountains.*

Sunday, September 20, 1863.

*After an exceedingly cold night the morning breaks damp
and very misty.*

*Marched at 6 AM after crossing two high ridges had a very
pleasant bottom road until we reached the Cumberland
Mountains.*

---

[96] Private Samuel Eyer was recruited from Centre County and mustered
into Co. E on September 15, 1861. Eyer remained with the regiment but was
absent due to illness at the mustering out of the regiment in 1865.

[97] Private David E. Bowen was recruited from Tiago County and
mustered into Co. G on September 18, 1861. Bowen was promoted to Sergeant
on January 1, 1865. Wounded at Petersburg, Virginia on April 2, 1865, Bowen
recovered and mustered out with his company on July 17, 1865.

About 10.30 we reached the famous Gap, so recently occupied by our forces, & soon scaled the height, numerous small earthworks are to be seen but the natural strength of the position is so great that [illegible] need add but little. At the summit of the Gap stands a square stone marking the boundary of KY, Tenn & Virg, which here meet. Stepping forward we enter east Tennessee & commence our descent. Some captured guns & more earthworks are to be seen, the ruins of a mill on the left we pass on. Camping about 1 ½ miles from the Gap, in an apple orchard.

Monday, September 21, 1863.

Contrary to yesterday's expectations we are again on the early move today, dispatches for us to hurry on having been received in the night. The day is beautiful and the country through which we pass is also good though somewhat broken and mountainous. Some beautiful scenery we meet, and cross one fine stream, Powell's river, by a rough bridge, reached Janewell, the county seat of Clairborne between 10 & 11 AM. & halted for coffee, this had once been a fine well built town, but its best buildings are now in ruins, the work of the rebels, I am told. There is a more thrifty appearance in general as we pass along, than in Southern Kentucky, fruit & others crops good, & most excellent water abundant. Camped about 2 ½ miles from the Clinch river, having marched 18 miles.

Tuesday, September 22, 1863.

In motion about 5 AM, the day is beautiful & morning not so cold as yesterday, between 6 & 7 AM we reached & forded the Clinch river, a rapid & rocky mountainous stream, wide & difficult to ford. Saw a specimen of "dog fish" caught in it (Allegheny Hellvenda)—After the river we crossed two mountains, one the Clinch was the highest & most difficult we have met, the descent on the South side almost impassible for wagons, halted for coffee at the base of mountain & resumed our march at 1.20 PM, forded the Holston river, a larger than the Clinch between 4 & 5 PM. & reached camp near Morristown after dark. Marched 21 miles, teams not up, and write this by the camp fire at midnight, must remain to keep warm.

The view from Clinch Mt is magnificent.

Wednesday, September 23, 1863.

Clear and warm. Wagon train came up all night.

Lay quietly in camp until about noon, when marching orders were received.

The 3rd Brig. & the wagon train of the Division left, the troops taking cars for Gainesville and train the road. Many strange rumors are afloat. Went to Morristown and found no transportation for us, so returned to camp again, & employed the remainder of the afternoon in picking Chinkapin, which are abundant. Slept by the fire on some straw, tents all gone.

Thursday, September 24, 1863.

Clear and very warm, everything takes another course today. Wagon train back on the Knoxville road after leaving been 11 miles towards Gainesville. The 3rd Brigade returned & went down on the car last night. Left Morristown in afternoon & marched over good but very dusty roads to Mosey Creek, passing by Panther Spring, encamped after 5 P.M. and did not turn in until late.

Gen Burnside was in M— this morning. Came in camp fresh & fine.

Water is becoming scarce but still continues excellent in quality, cold & delicious.

Friday, September 25, 1863.

Arose this morning with headache, pains in limbs & a general feeling of lassitude.

Marched with difficulty. Halted for coffee at noon at Strawberry Plains on the Hulston, where we found a union demonstration in progress.

The East Tennessean's seem a different people from those of other southern states. Much more friendly, but the planter class generally Secesh, while the log cabin is the home of the union man.

Was taken with severe chill followed by fever, after dinner and with great difficulty reached camp, crossed the river on ferry.

Saturday, September 26, 1863.

After passing quite a comfortable night at the house of a farmer near by, (our wagon train not coming up) I was aroused about daylight, after breakfast I followed the regiment taking my own time as I did not feel very strong.

No particular occurrence on the march, arrived in camp near Knoxville about noon. Shortly after had a return of chill & fever which occupied the afternoon. In the evening I received from WHP-. The clothing &c sent from home by Bro Will. All coming in good season & of most excellent material also a fine handkerchief from SRG—. All very

*welcome indeed, as the season for their use is fast
approaching.*

Sunday, September 27, 1863.

*A bright and warm day. Visited Knoxville and attended
Presbyterian Church in morning, found the town quite large
& well built, having evidently been a thriving place in times
of Peace. The Pastor & Congregation are secesh, have a
magnificent church but there endeth the matter. Back to
camp at noon & in after had the same old chill & fever.*

Commenced a free use of Quinine.

*A welcome old friend the mail has turned up again, brings
me a letter from Bro Ed—*

Monday, September 28, 1863.

*A quiet day in camp and not feeling at all well I keep quiet
myself keeping of the chill & fever with Quinine.*

*Recd a letter from SBG— who is again at Cin Hospl and
doing very well.*

Tuesday, September 29, 1863.

*Quiet as yesterday.Suffer much with headache but have
broken the fever, & came near breaking my head with
Quinine.*

Wednesday, September 30, 1863.

Am getting better slowly but feel dull and weak.

*Our old commander Genl Burnside visited our camp & was
heartily welcomed by all, he seems glad to see us and proud
too of the old 9th Boy's—.*

Thursday, October 1, 1863.

Opens wet, and proves a wet autumn day. We lie under cover and keep dry.

I am reading, "True to last, or Alone on the Wide Wide Sea," by AS. Roe.[98] *A most interesting & instructive work.*

Friday, October 2, 1863.

Opens cloudy, by noon clear and pleasant.

A quiet day, very little stirring.

Saturday, October 3, 1863.

Aroused early by orders for our Brigade to march at 8 AM. In light order with 5 days rations, take the cars for Morristown where it seems guerillas have been appearing.

Brigade left on time, but I am left in charge of our baggage &c a few sick men are left on hand, mostly chill fever cases.

Wrote to Bro ETM & Mrs Truman.

Visited Knoxville in afternoon.

Sunday, October 4, 1863.

A quiet Sunday, the camp is deserted and still, very lonesome with nothing to do. Wrote to SRG—. And had a visit from M.A.C—

The day is beautifully clear and pleasant followed by a cold night, making us think winter is coming on rapidly.

---

[98] *True to the Last; or, Alone On A Wide, Wide Sea* (1858) by A.S. Roe.

Monday, October 5, 1863.

A beautiful autumn morning, cool and bracing—the bright sky changing to a cold leaden here.

Wrote to WAM & SWK—. Our Sutler Starr came in today, bringing quite a supply of sundries, amongst others Butter, which was soon caught up at 60¢.

Tuesday, October 6, 1863.

Opens clear and bright. A quiet day, little stirring was at division Head Quarters in afternoon in search of Quinine which is becoming scarce. The day closes dull & heavy with prospects of rain—.

Wednesday, October 7, 1863.

Opens wet, a cold, damp October day—.

Thursday, October 8, 1863.

Overcast with a cold N.W. wind—.

Friday, October 9, 1863.

All goes quietly in the camp.

Saturday, October 10, 1863.

A pleasant day, Q.M. Sergt Mullen returned from the front bringing me a letter from Dr C- who reports all quiet, and desires a number of articles sent to him. An engagement with the enemy is daily anticipated. Genl Burnside has gone to the front.

Sunday, October 11, 1863.

A beautiful day, cool and pleasant, in morning attended church in Knoxville, in afternoon wrote to SRG, otherwise the day has been quiet. After retiring in evening learned that our regiment yesterday losing 2 killed & 17 wounded, the killed were 1st Serg McMichael[99] of Co C— & Whitmore[100] of Co G—, the wounded have arrived in Camp.[101]

Monday, October 12, 1863.

A quiet and pleasant day, in evening recd a large mail bringing me letters from S.A.M. W.H.M. & SRG—. Our first mail in weeks. We hear more of the particulars of the fight and learn that our boys have behaved nobly, adding fresh honors to those already won.

Tuesday, October 13, 1863.

Rain! Rain! A real election day, and our thoughts wander off to 'Old Keystone' as we feel anxious for the results of the election today, hoping that the Union course may triumph and Gov Curtin be re-elected. Wrote to Sallie A.M. in evening enclosing a pay master's check for $75.— to be placed to my account, also wrote to Lizzie Truman.

---

[99] 1st Sergeant George McMichaels was recruited from Mifflin County and mustered into service on August 31, 1861. McMichaels was promoted to 1st Sergeant on July 7, 1863. On October 10, 1863 McMichaels was killed at Blue Springs, Tennessee.

[100] Private Chester Whitmore [Wetmore] was recruited from Tiago County and mustered into service on September 18, 1861. Whitmore was killed at Blue Springs, Kentucky on October 10, 1863.

[101] The Battle of Blue Springs, Tennessee fought on October 10, 1863 between Union forces under Major General Ambrose Burnside and Confederate forces under Brigadier General John Stuart Williams' (1818-1898). The battle was a Union victory.

Wednesday, October 14, 1863.

The counterpart of yesterday rain falling in showers.

Another mail in afternoon, by which I received a letter from WHG—Salem Ohio.

Was much surprised after turning in for the night to find our regiment came shambling through the dark into camp—an unexpected return to all.

The boys seem heartily glad to get back to the old camp—

Thursday, October 15, 1863.

Over cast with some rain. Camp is lively to-day with scrubbing up after the hard tramp. Put up hospital tent, and opened out for a stay—.

Heavy rain in evening & through the night—.

Friday, October 16, 1863.

Opens wet and very unpleasant.

Saturday, October 17, 1863.

Clear and very pleasant.

Visited Knoxville and the Asylum Hospital where our wounded men are lying was not much pleased with the condition of things there. Afterward had my Ambrotype taken.

Parson Brownlow & the Hon H. Maynard loyal refugees from K— returned yesterday & speak in the Court House to-night.

Sunday, October 18, 1863.

Opens with high winds and soon proves a wet and disagreeable day.

Corpl R. Bailey died at Asylum Hospl this mon'g he was wounded in the fight of the 10th—

By the mail in evening received a letter from Sister dated 7th.

By order of Lt Col Hills Hospl Attendants D. Bower and S. Eyer were returned to their companies.

Monday, October 19, 1863.

Opens wet and disagreeable, growing somewhat colder and more like our Autumn at home, towards noon cleared off bright and pleasant.

Received marching orders with 10 days rations to-morrow.

Tuesday, October 20, 1863.

Clear and bright.

Broke camp and took up our line of march southward, leaving Knoxville at 8 A.M—. Passed through a beautiful and well cultivated valley. Stopped at noon for coffee, when we heard cannonading in advance towards Loudon.

Resuming our march at 3.15 PM. We reached camp for the night at 5.15 P.M. having marched about 15 miles, wagon train came up in good season—.

Wednesday, October 21, 1863.

Reveille at 3.30 AM—A mild damp morning an occasional gun still booms out in our advance—. This day is the second anniversary of the organization of our regiment, two years out from Camp Curtin.

Camped shortly before noon about 4 miles from Loudon, after marching through a pelting rain.

Wagons up late in afternoon. Secured plenty of straw and had a comfortable night—.

Thursday, October 22, 1863.

Opens cloudy but cleared away towards noon and proved warm. Lay quiet until 2 PM. Then marched to Loudon & crossed the river on Pontoon, camping near the town.

The country hereabout is much broken and hilly, many strong positions some of which are fortified—, presenting as we approached the river a strong resemblance to the vicinity of Frederiksberg VA.

Friday, October 23, 1863.

Opens wet with thunder shower, which settled into a steady rain which lasted all day, making everything disagreeable almost hemming us in with mud made the best of it lying quiet under shelter.

Saturday, October 24, 1863.

Cloudy with a cold wind. Marching orders at noon, broke camp and sent sick & baggage across the river. Gen Burnside has arrived and every thing promises a speady engagement with the enemy. An occasional heavy gun in the distance booms out, lay all afternoon ready to march at a moment's notice but night found us yet in the old camp—

Struck up a shelter of rails & gum blankets under which we spent a comfortable and quiet night.

Sunday, October 25, 1863.

Opens cold and partially clear. The retreat which was anticipated last night did not occur, time drags wearily on while waiting further orders. Attended divine service at Brig Head Quarters the Chaplin of 79th N.Y. officiating, had an excellent discourse,—the Chaplin in young & just from home, very earnest and bids fair to make a useful officer—.

Monday, October 26, 1863.

The weather is becoming mild again. A year ago today since with the Army of the Potomac we entered Virginia crossing the Potomac at Berlin Md—

Our wagon train remains on the other side of the river, but some of the baggage has been brought us and we again have a tent.

A [illegible] beautiful moonlight night, calm and pleasant—

Tuesday, October 27, 1863.

Opens damp and chilly with a little rain. The rations continue short, and a very stringent order against foraging on the country has been issued by Genl Burnside.

Attended the funeral of a Sergt of the 80 Ills Vols in afternoon.

Evening brings us marching orders for the morrow, a start before daylight & things savor of retreat.

More than one half of our regiment is on Picket today—.

Wednesday, October 28, 1863.

After a restless night up at 2.30 AM. Pack up an send off tent—but the troops did not move until about day break.

The morning is foggy & damp. No Reveille or drum beat this morning everything goes quietly & under cover of darkness & the heavy mist, daybreak found us crossing the Pontoon again, when we found that the whole force in motion.

London was evacuated all the troops withdrawn across the river.

In afternoon went into camp near Lenoir's Station & East Tenn & Ga RRd—. Received a letter from SBG—Camp Dennison Ohio.

Thursday, October 29, 1863.

Opens foggy & damp, but clears up warm & bright towards noon. After dinner changed camp & obtained an excellent location in woods, where we received orders to go into winter quarters.

Wrote to WAM & enclosed my picture which I had taken at Knoxville.

Already the ringing of the ax is through the woods tells that the huts are progress.

Friday, October 30, 1863.

Opens wet and gives us a day of rain, yet had a busy day in the woods cutting out timber for my hut—

Saturday, October 31, 1863.

Muster day, but as clothing & c is all in disorder there was no Inspection, the Major of 36th Mass was mustering officer—.

Spent the afternoon on grinding axes ready to work on the framing up of the house—.

Received a letter of Oct 11th from SRG—.

Sunday, November 1, 1863.

Opens clear and cold we hope now our season of wet has passed by—. Put up the Hospl tent.— Capt S. Wright of Genl Potter's Staff visited us today, brought a "Spy" of 17th latest home date.

Dropped my watch in the woods, but was fortunate enough to regain it with a cracked crystal—.

Large mail in evening letters from S.A.M 19th S.R.G 19th & CEG-22nd.

Monday, November 2, 1863.

Commenced work framing the cabin in good earnest the progress is slow but sure.

Tuesday, November 3, 1863.

The cabin progresses finely, have little else to do but work upon it. The exercise is excellent and give a real wood choppers appetite.

Wednesday, November 4, 1863.

The greater portion of today was consumed in working on the cabin chimney, lined the fire place with brick and mudded up the remainder of the chimney, by evening had a roaring fire in it little else remains to be done except adding the roof.

Thursday, November 5, 1863.

The sky threatens rain and before noon it is upon us, but we have the roof on and mind it but little. Already we begin to experience the comforts of the new home—.

Put up a bed stand of poplar hewed out today, and have a bed of corn husks. Sleep in the cabin to-night for first time.

Friday, November 6, 1863.

Opens bright and clear the weather is mild and pleasant for the season—

The chimney of the Hospital was commenced today.

Saturday, November 7, 1863.

Bright yet keen and cold in the morning—. Today a year ago we experienced the first snow of the season at Orleans Va, marched through the storm to Carter's Creek. Spent the day in policing & cleaning up generally.

Wrote to SRG—in evg.

Sunday, November 8, 1863.

Opens bright and pleasant but becomes overcast with rough wind towards noon—.

General Inspection of the regiment by the Insp Genl was the only one of the N.C.S out—.

Wrote to S.A.M & Robt Woods—and in Atlantic Monthly Jan'y 1862 read a most interesting & instructive article entitled Jefferson & Slavery.

Quite a large mail this morning but nothing for me.

Monday, November 9, 1863.

Overcast cold and raw old winter seems hovering around, and this afternoon dropped a few reminders in the way of snowflakes the first we have seen.

Tuesday, November 10, 1863.

After a cold night the day opens foggy, but the sun soon dispels the fog and gives a beautiful day—.

Wrote to W.H.G—

Late in evening received orders to be ready to march at daylight tomorrow.

Wednesday, November 11, 1863.

Roused by an early reveille, regiment in line and stacked before day, it proved but a precautionary movement. A pontoon having thrown across the river & we were held in readiness for support if needed but the day passed quickly and evening found us still in our old camp.

By mail in evening a letter from Mrs T—. also one in my came from Sam G—. from which I judge that he is on his way here, hope it may be so.

Thursday, November 12, 1863.

Opens clear and bright, we are having cold frosty nights, but pleasant days—.

Wrote to Peterson & Bro Philada for books enclosing $2.00—

Friday, November 13, 1863.

A mild pleasant day.

Snow—our Sutler arrived bringing in a large stock of goods—purchased a pair of boots from him, price $10.00—

Am reading 'Waverly'[102] by 'Scott' & am much interested in it—.

Saturday, November 14, 1863.

Opens foggy and damp and finally have heavy rain—. About 4 AM received orders to be ready to move at daylight— everything indicates a skedaddle and transportation is very limited—. Many conflicting orders and rumors are about which causes much trouble.

Move at 12 AM. Wagon train going towards K—. & we head to London—have a very hard march through rain & mud, reach the river in time to witness but not participate in skirmish. Enemy across in force, march until after dark and lay by our fires, expecting to make a night attack—. A cold wet night with little sleep—

---

[102] *Waverly; or, 'Tis Sixty Years Since* (1814) by Sir Walter Scott

137

Sunday, November 15, 1863.

Under way before daylight—retracing our yesterdays steps. Another hard pull back to Lenoir, go into position, 23 pickets of 8th Mich captured in very short time—. Sharp firing—Our whole division went in to line of battle our brigade in the front in which position they remained until a few hours before day break, early in the night an alarm was given the enemy having made a dash on rear pickets after which the night passed quietly[103]

Monday, November 16, 1863.

Long before day up and stir, retreat seems the order of the day. A large number of wagons & great amount of baggage & stores were destroyed & abandoned, much private baggage amongst the lost.

The enemy at day break discovering our retreat passed in closely and our rear guard was soon engaged. I cannot describe the day's events, the march through roads of the worst possible condition. Near Campbell's Station, a halt was made & a severe fight ensued, but we held the enemy in check until after night then under cover of darkness, again fall back, reaching Knoxville about 4 AM, much exhausted. 23 ½ miles & a tough fight, for this day's work. Our regiment lost about 20 men.[104]

---

[103] Battle of Lenoir's Station, Tennessee, fought on November 14-15, 1863 between Union forces under Major General Ambrose Burnside and Confederate forces under Lieutenant General James Longstreet. The battle was a Confederate victory, with Burnside's forces retreating to Campbell's Station, Tennessee.

[104] Battle of Campbell's Station, Tennessee, fought on November 16, 1863, between Union forces under Major General Ambrose Burnside and Confederate forces under Lieutenant General James Longstreet. The battle was a Union victory.

Tuesday, November 17, 1863.

The weather is damp cold & raw. Awoke this morning cold & stiff, hungry with little to eat, here we make a stand. Some fine position are in our hands, for three days we have been on the go with little to eat and marching over wretched roads a great part in the dark.

Our regt supports the 2nd N.Y. battery in position at the College of E. Ten, during the afternoon some sharp skirmishing goes on but the enemy cannot pass in our lines, a great fight may be expected here.

Tonight camp in the college building & hope to have a nights sleep.[105]

As most of our baggage was destroyed, I have lost everything except what I have carried in my knapsack.

Wednesday, November 18, 1863.

Opens with a very heavy fog—the night passed quietly—In the morning reported at Asylum Hospital—nothing doing in afternoon, the Court House was taken as Hospl for 9th Corps & arranged as such.

Considerable skirmishing & some artillery firing occurred through the day but our Corps met with little loss.

A general engagement is hourly expected, & may occur either by day or night—.

Had a long hunt for cook stove & finally succeeded after much trouble among rebel women & others.

---

[105] East Tennessee University, founded in 1794 as Blount College. During the Siege of Knoxville, Tennessee the university would be used as barracks and hospital for Union soldiers.

Thursday, November 19, 1863.

Opens foggy & gives a mild & pleasant day, the Skirmishing continues but we have little loss & consequently little to do—. Many rumors circulate, but we are all confident of Genl B's ability to hold our present position, both sides are busy entrenching. Genl Saunders of 23rd Corps, wounded yesterday, died today & was buried to-night.

Friday, November 20, 1863.

Weather continues mild & things in general seem in status quo.

Towards evening have a slight rain.

Early in the night the town was illuminated by the burning of a number of buildings which the enemy used as shelter for sharp shooters.

Several companies of 17th Mich charged the enemies rifle pits, held them & burned several homes retired with a loss of two killed & 3 slightly wounded—.

Saturday, November 21, 1863.

Opens with heavy rain, which proves the order of the day. Only two cases on our table today an amputation of right leg above the knee, and a broken lower jaw.

Sunday, November 22, 1863.

A bright and pleasant Sunday morning. Provisions seem getting scarce, are down on ½ rations bread and pork, no coffee or sugar.

A case of resection of lower jaw was on our table this morning. Operation performed by Dr Coggswell of 29th Mass.

Monday, November 23, 1863.

A mild pleasant day.

Two couriers arrived from the Gap this morning. A very quiet day. In the even'g city was again illuminated by the burning of buildings outside our lines, to prevent their occupation by rebel sharp shooters.

An amputation of right arm on our table this ev'g.

Tuesday, November 24, 1863.

Opens with fog, and sharp skirmishing on our left of centre. The 2nd Mich Regt charged the rebel rifle pits, carried them but for want of support had to retire, their lose was 89 killed, wounded & missing. The mist of the morning has changed to rain making a disagreeable day.

The day has proved a busy one. After dark a few who had been wounded in the morning and laid concealed until nightfall, then made their way within our lines. The Hospital is rapidly filling up. The horrors of war are every where around us, we all anxiously await the day when this terrible ordeal shall have passed. The enemy practice their old game of stripping the dead who fall into their hands. Rations of tobacco were issued today.

Wednesday, November 25, 1863.

Opens bright, clear and quite cold.

The siege progresses slowly, an occasional wounded man is brought in, most of the wounds are of a serious character. Among others were Cap't Wilksin 20th Mich, shot in back & spine injured, lower extremities paralyzed. Lieut Col Comstock, 17th Mich Vols shot in chest, died about midnight, both fine men.

Thursday, November 26, 1863.

Thanksgiving day opens clear and cold—by way of a Thanksgiving dinner we have a bit of baked beef, a sumptuous meal for us.

One man, Gates[106] of Co E from our regiment wounded in rifle pits this afternoon, wound considered mortal.

Friday, November 27, 1863.

Cool and bright.

Visited our regiment in afternoon and found then quite well situated in what had been the winter camp of the 104th Ohio.

Signed pay rolls for pay to Nov 1st 1863, including clothing acct $70.29—

Two men brought in wounded and several died. About three deaths a day is our average. So many of the wounded are serious that we may find many more dying.

The evening is damp & we may anticipate rain.

---

[106] Private Caleb Gates was recruited from Centre County and mustered into Company E of the 45th Pennsylvania Volunteers on September 15, 1861. Gates died on December 6, 1863 from his wounds.

Saturday, November 28, 1863.

Opens with rain, which gives a dull day, with little doing outside of regular Hospital routines.

Towards evening the wind increased blowing strong from north west, cold & raw.

Sunday, November 29, 1863.

Opens raw and cold.

The past night has witnessed a determined attempt on the part of the Rebels to drive us out of some of our strong positions, in which the met with a most signal failure. In front of Fort Sanders their loss was particularly heavy. One desperate charge was made on the fort in which they reached the ramparts but were hurled back with terrific slaughter, & with the loss of numerous prisoners.

There was more or less fighting all night all night long, but the greatest portion was about day light.

We had plenty of work at the Hospital, but mostly among the rebel wounded of whom we had a large share.

In afternoon, under a flag of truce most of the wounded were transferred into their lines. Twelve regiments (Georgians & Miss) were represented among the wounded. A few of our men were returned.

Monday, November 30, 1863.

Clear and cold, the day has passed very quiet in the front. An occasional exchange of shots and a few men wounded, seventy killed. Winter seems upon us in earnest, the cold is very trying on the men in the front yet we hear little or no complaints, all are cheerful. Five deaths in Hospital is the last 24 hours, not including several rebel dead.

Tuesday, December 1, 1863.

The weather continues clear and very cold.

Visited the regiment in the front this morning and found all going quietly with them. More rumors are afoot.

Wednesday, December 2, 1863.

Weather is moderating but continues clear.

There is little outside of what has become the regular routine stirring. We have plenty of rumors afloat and some on seeming good authority. Help is coming and we trust our days of beleauguerment are drawing to a close, for several nights past another attack has been anticipated but none has occurred.

An occasional wounded man is brought in.

The mortality of the Hospital has been greater than usual.

Time passes rapidly we are already in the third week of the siege, and can hold out quite a while yet. We very much miss our mails & communication with home, where the friends must be anxious for our welfare—.

Thursday, December 3, 1863.

Opens bright clear and pleasant. Our dead house has eight occupants this morning. One killed on the field, the others died in Hospital. During the night we have had considerable cannonading, sounding more like signaling than anything else.

My line of duty has been changed again today, from the operating room I go into the Dispensary and take charge there. Keeping the register &c promises to be a bust position and I think to my liking. Have a pleasant room for and office, Dr Fox of 8ᵗʰ Michigan is now in charge of Hospital, things are gradually coming in shape.

There has been nothing unusual about the front today, the impression that the enemy is leaving seems to be gaining ground.

Friday, December 4, 1863.

Opens bright and pleasant the weather has become quite moderate again. But one death during the past 24 hours, a colored servant of 50ᵗʰ P.V.

There is some firing about the front, but no engagement, two wounded men were brought in. Reinforcements have arrived and the siege is now virtually raised—unless the Rebs skedaddle they will hear from us inside of 24 hours. Our turn now to act an offensive.

I have passed a busy day.

Saturday, December 5, 1863.

Opens cloudy and gives us our Saturday's rain, making the 4ᵗʰ raining Saturday.

The night has passed very quietly, one death in Hospital.

On examination it was found that our loving friends the Rebs, have given up the siege & skedaddled. An attack was to have been made on the today. Prisoners are coming in quite plenty.

Wrote to S.A.M & S.R.G.

Sunday, December 6, 1863.

A pleasant and mild day—In morning visited a deserted mansion within what had been the Rebel lines in search of anything that might prove useful in Hospital. Passed over some of the Confederate ground, visited the ruins of the house destroyed by the 17th Mich in this gallant charge. Found war's grim & disabling footsteps everywhere around. The country for miles around has become a barren wilderness. The citizens are beginning to hunt up their desolated homes, in many instances to find but a mass of ruins. Rebel prisoners are being brought in in great numbers, their wounded in hospitals were deserted and remain in our hands among are found some of our boys who were wounded & prisoners.

Monday, December 7, 1863.

Opens with heavy fog and damp & chilly. A chase is being made after the enemy & our division joins in, in light marching order, the boys notwithstanding their recent hardships and short rations moved off cheerily seeming in good spirits at the change. Things about town are beginning to resume their wonted work, but rations yet continue short, only by purchasing where ever to be found & at high prices can we keep appetite supplied, but the quality seems to be improving.

On connection with the steward of 20th Mich I am detailed to remain at this Division Hospl & may have a long siege of it. Am acting in capacity of Clerk & Dispenser, have a pleasant office & plenty to keep me employed, but hope after things are righted to have matters easier. Recd my pay to Nov 1st

63, including clothing a/e—$70.29, paid Sutler a/e $4.05, purchased gold per for $2.00.

Tuesday, December 8, 1863.

Opens cold and raw, have rain about 10 AM—which continues more or less all day—Have had a very busy day almost more than I could go thro' with, as I feel quite unwell have a sore mouth & throat.

More duties added to mine am made Commissary for Hospitals of 1st & 2nd Divs have the funding of about 230 men and little to [illegible] with—. My pen keeps going more now than I like.

Quite a good serenade to-night by a brass band.

Wednesday, December 9, 1863.

Mild and pleasant. The town is full of fresh troops & many have been passing through on their way to reinforce our Army after Longstreet. My commissary matters keep me very busy. The parties who conducted it before do not seem inclined to give me much information, & I have to depend much on my own exertions to ascertain to condition of affairs, one thing is certain, the boys all have had enough to eat today, without hunting up outside things at enormous prices. The diet for the patients is not sufficient.

Thursday, December 10, 1863.

Partially overcast but yet a pleasant day. The city has been thronged with country folk, coming in to see friends in a Tenn Brig that came in yesterday, but passed on. Still have a big rush of business. Got in quite a lot of delicacies for our wounded & sick.

There has been a good deal of storm about the establishment today but to-night seems quiet.

Hospital was serenaded by an excellent Brass Band this afternoon. The sanitary condition of Hospital is improving deaths are few. An occasional wounded man who had been a prisoner comes in.

Friday, December 11, 1863.

Mild and pleasant.

A very busy day for me, but that is nothing unusual for me now.

Made my first return to Commissary for Hospital today.

Wrote to Bro Will giving him a descriptions of adventures during siege.

Major Byington of the 2nd Mich died today.

Saturday, December 12, 1863.

Weather continues mild but promises rain, have things reduced to more system and getting along easier.

The sanitary condition of our hospital is improving.

Sunday, December 13, 1863.

Opens wet.

A large mail in brings me a letter from S.B.G. and a pair of mittens from WHG—. Had a glance at two home local papers of October, and a Cin paper of Dec 1st.

A few apples are to be had about town at from 50¢ to $1.00 per dozen, small at that.

Heavy rain at night.

Monday, December 14, 1863.

Opens raw & cold, with high winds.

Nothing particular stirring, received letter from W.H.G S.AM & WHM, the two latter nearly a month old.

Wrote to S.B.G—.

Tuesday, December 15, 1863.

A mild and pleasant day—News from the front indicate work to do there, reinforcements are being sent out.[107]

Still have a bothering time with Commissary.

A large detachment of Rebel prisoners were sent off north today.

Wednesday, December 16, 1863.

The weather continues mild and pleasant—.

Our Corps Commissary is ordered to the front & we have to draw from the post, more difficulty.

---

[107] Battle of Bean's Station, Tennessee, fought on December 14, 1863 between Union forces under Major General John Parke (1827-1900) and Brigadier General James M. Shackelford (1827-1909) against Confederate forces under Lieutenant General James Longstreet. The battle was a Confederate victory. The Siege of Knoxville ended after the Battle of Bean's Station with both sides going into winter quarters.

More reinforcements have gone to the front & we may expect an engagement there, our forces have fallen back nearer the city.

A number of wounded from the front brought into town today.

Thursday, December 17, 1863.

Opens damp—had heavy during the night.

Later in the day the wind rose and gave us a rough windy day—and tonight the wind howls wildly round.

Recd letter from EJ.M SR.G LSJ & EG.T—

More reinforcements passed on to the front today.

From Mrs Truman, received a neat little flag breast pin.

Drew coffee today for the first time in weeks, the boys are all glad to have our old friend back again.

A few Sanitary stores arrived today, much needed & most welcome. Mr Francis from Western Penna is here by authority of Gov C— visiting our wounded & sick Penna Boys.

Friday, December 18, 1863.

Opens cold—a good bracing day reminding one of our northern homes. Still have plenty to do, kept on the go all day—

All regimental baggage ordered to the front—sent Dr C's baggage & the boys knapsacks—

Saturday, December 19, 1863.

We are having winter in earnest—Old Boreas is howling about—though cold the weather is fine & clear—

Have had another busy day—the sick of our Div who had been left in convalescent camp have been transported here and we are having big arrivals.

Our hospital has been made a General Hospital & is now styled U.S Genl Hospital No 5, Court House Knoxville.

Sunday, December 20, 1863.

The weather continues clear & cold, had promised myself a day of rest today but find it unusually busy, the arrivals from the Convalescent Camp are greater than expected & create some confusion. Dr Fox received notice tonight that he had been relieved & Dr Cogswell of the 29th Mass placed in charge of our hospital—We are all sorry to part with Dr F. he having worked with us all faithfully & well.

Dr C- is also a good officer.

Charlie Gardner drummer boy of 8th Mich. Died of wounds.

Monday, December 21, 1863.

We are still having bright clear weather. I am sure the boys in the front are glad for it—as they are much exposed.

Attending the funeral of Charlie the drummer, he was buried with the honors of war—and in absence of other music, had the Highland bag pipes of the 79th NY—, there was a large attendance at the funeral, as Charlie had ever been a pet—. An appropriate address was delivered at the grave, by Mr Francis of Penna—. Dr Cogswell arrived this evening, some new arrangements will now be made—and I hope to have matters somewhat easier.

Tuesday, December 22, 1863.

The weather continues clear and bright, but is moderating. We have many statements from our division saying that a great portion of the old 3 years men are re-enlisting in the Veteran Corps.

The inmates of the Hospl presented Surgn Fox with an over coat & pair gauntlets on his retiring from the charge of Hospl.

Wednesday, December 23, 1863.

Opens clouded, damp & raw—Dr Fox left for front this morning, also a number of convalescents.

Wrote to SR.G—& EGM.

There have been several mails of late but no mail for me—.

Thursday, December 24, 1863.

The weather continues clear & fine—.

Squads of prisoners are arriving today—some little fighting has been going on in front.

Night before Christmas what pleasant memories come up— and pleasant would be to be at home at this festive season here we have nothing to remind us of the time.

Friday, December 25, 1863.

Christmas day—opens over cast and raw it being ration day I have a busy morning—Do not feel very well, have throughout a very dull day—

By way of having something homelike bought a quart of chestnuts for which I paid 40¢—. Gave the wounded & sick as good a dinner as could be raised.

Poultry & sweet potatoes.

Saturday, December 26, 1863.

Opens with rain—and gives a wet day.

Sunday, December 27, 1863.

Another wet day—filling our streets with mud—the only quiet Sunday I have had for weeks—wrote to Sister SAM, and to WNG—

Some new arrangements in our messing in connection with the other Stewards commenced messing in the officers mess room, have our rations served up more regularly & in a better manner—.

Monday, December 28, 1863.

Opens with rain again, have a busy morning, around here and there.

Received quite a supply of sanitary stores most welcome and much needed. Here if anywhere such supplies find a good field, and could but the kind contributors of the north see the benefits of their gifts, I'm sure they would feel richly repaid—.

Tuesday, December 29, 1863.

A clear and beautiful day.

Busy hunting up a wagon for foraging, catbagged a spring wagon & extra pairs of wheels—.

Wrote to Mrs Truman.

Wednesday, December 30, 1863.

Mild and pleasant the old year is going out quietly— Received another supply of sanitary goods—we are doing very well.

Thursday, December 31, 1863.

Plenty rain and mud, have much outdoor traveling, after Poultry &c obtained quite a fine stock and can give quite a New Year's dinner.

The evening is wild and stormy—heavy rain & wind, the old year struggles as it dies.

News from the front say that the boys are re-enlisting rapidly, the prospects are that our regiment will go ¾ or more & I am quite exercised about it & may take the fever.

1864

January 1st, 1864—[108]

The new year opens with a roaring NW-wind the coldest morning we have had—The day passed rather pleasantly, had a good New Years dinner—

Visited some of the fortifications around the city.

Rations day—drew beans for the first time in Tenn, a great treat.

Jany 2, 1864[109]

Having obtained permission to visit the front, started after waiting at the RRd from 9 AM until after 3 P.M. finally got off—arrived at Strawberry Plains at sunset and had 8 miles to tramp over the roughest imaginable road in the dark— arrived at camp about "Taps," was heartily welcomed by the troops & passed quite a comfortable night in a shelter tent by the fire—weather cloudy & threatens snow.

Sunday, Jany 3rd 1864

Up in season, the day is cloudy but the weather moderating. Around thru' the camp and find the boys cheerful & very enthusiastic on their re enlistment nearly the entire number have gone into it and of course when so many of my old

---

[108] Pocket diaries are designed with slots designated for each day of the year. While in Knoxville, Tennessee, James Meyers completed his 1863 diary. Unable to obtain a new diary, Meyers continued to record his daily events in the memorandum section of the 1863 diary. Meyers ended the entries on January 27, 1864.

[109] I have reproduced how James Meyers wrote the dates for the entries of January 1864.

comrades lend off I will not be behind. So this afternoon was mustered in for 3 years more as H.S.

Finished up the rest of my business & am ready to start back tomorrow, prospects for a home trip are bright—. A slight sprinkling of snow tonight—

Monday, Jany 4th 1864

After a soldiers breakfast start in the rain for the RRD at the plains & arrived in time for train after many delays we reach K— about 3 P.M. back again to the Hospital & to work—the weather is wet and road muddy.

Tuesday 5th

Weather continues cold, growing colder with appearances of snow. Wrote to SBG—& WHM.

Wednesday Jan'y 6th 1864

Opens cold & clouded, giving us quite a dash of snow, which gives the country quite a country appearance—Rations day drew for 300 men.

Thursday Jany 7th 1864

Cold and clouded with quite a fall of snow in evening covering the ground to the depth of several inches.

Had a note from M.A.C—informing me of his re-enlistment.

Friday, Jany 8th 1864

Opens bright and clear, the country wears a wintry appearance with its robe of white. E.S. Dodd 8th Texas Cavalry Rebel, was hung today as a spy, attended the execution, he died manfully without flinching. When the drop fell the rope broke, was again secured & the second attempt made which succeeded, on the site of this execution the rebels had hung a father & son (union) under very barbarous circumstances.

Tuesday, Jan'y 12th 1864

The past few days have gone quietly by—at my request I was this morning relieved from duty at Hospl No 5—& reported back to my regiment for duty—found all things going on as usual with the boys rations & clothing continue scarce—. The 100th & 50th Pa Vols started for home today.

Wednesday, Jany 13th 1864

Opens cold & cloudy, attended the morning sick call for the first time in two months. Signed my descriptive Rolls &c, &c am now certainly in for 3 years more—. The weather is growing milder—

Thursday, Jany 14th 1864

A clear, mild, & beautiful day.

Saturday, Jany 16th 1864

After two day's expectation we this morning broke camp and started on our homeward march. The day is beautiful & mild, ground is rapidly thawing out and the roads are wretchedly heavy, the boys march in good spirits. We have light haversacks but are looking ahead for plenty. Genl Wilcox met us on the way. Stopped & had a talk, he goes to command the old 9th.

Camped at night about 2 miles from the Clinch river, very tired & go to bed under the broad country—

Sunday, Jany 17th 1864

Opens cloudy, after a comfortable night on a bed of cedar, we are again on the march across Clinch river by Ferry—.

The road was exceedingly muddy & marching heavy camped for the night one mile from Tazewell pretty well tired.

Monday, Jany 18th 1864

Opens with rain. An early start and we pass through Tazewell winding through the mud's crossed Cumberland Gap and camp about 2 or 3 miles beyond toward evening, having marched about 17 miles.

Tuesday, Jany 19th 1864

On awakening find snow all about and on us, & driving in our faces, the rain having changed to snow, prospects for a tough march, we tug on and by noon have reached Cumberland ford having crossed three mountains. We past on and camp for the night ½ miles beyond Flat Look, having marched nearly 20 miles. Come in well used up—the snow squall has passed & we have a clear cold night.

Wednesday, Jany 20th 1864

Opens bright & pleasant woke up to find a hole burnt in my blanket having come to close to the fire.

Again moving & by 11.30 are in camp a Barboursville, made 8 miles over good road, the mud being frozen—.

Thursday, Jany 21st 1864

From Barboursville to one mile beyond the Big Laurel Bridge—

Friday, Jany 22nd 1864

Through London and camped at Little Rock Castle river—clear and cold—

Saturday, Jany 23rd '64

Across the Wild Cat mountains & Big Rock Castle river by Ferry boat to Mt Vernon a mild day & hard marching.

Sunday, Jany 24th 1864

A very mild and pleasant day—marched to about 3 miles beyond Crab Orchard out of the mountains & on good turnpike road, feel quite at home here.

Monday, Jany 25th 1864

Weather growing milder real spring like, through Lancaster to Camp Dick Robinson. Saw large numbers of fresh troops en route for Tennessee.

This is our tenth day we are now near RRd & will soon be home, have not been under shelter since leaving Blaines X road.

Tuesday, Jany 26th 1864

Bright & quite warm, marched from Camp Dick to Camp Nelson, halted for several hours picking up convalescents & sending in clothing estimates, then on to about 2½ miles of Nicholasville and camped for the night.

Jany 27, 1864

To Nicholasville & then by train to Covington ferry to Cincinnati and camped in open market house.

Poem copied into the July Cash Account section

A leaf that reminds of Thee
"How sweet is the hour we give,
When fancy may wander free,
To the friends who memory live! –
For then I remember thee!
Then, winged, like the dove from the air
My head o'er a stormy sea,
Bring back to my lonely bank
A leaf that reminds of thee!
II

But still does the sky look dark
The waters still deep and wide
Oh: when may my lonely bank
In peace on the shore abide?
But through the future far,
Dark through my course may be,
Thou art my guiding star!
My heart still turns to thee!
III

When I see thy friends I smile,
Sigh when I hear thy name;
But they cannot tell the while
Whence the smile or sadness came,
Vainly the world may deem
The course of my sighs they know:
The breeze that ruffles the stream
Knows not the depth below."

Knoxville Tenn Oct 9th 1863

Part Two: 1865

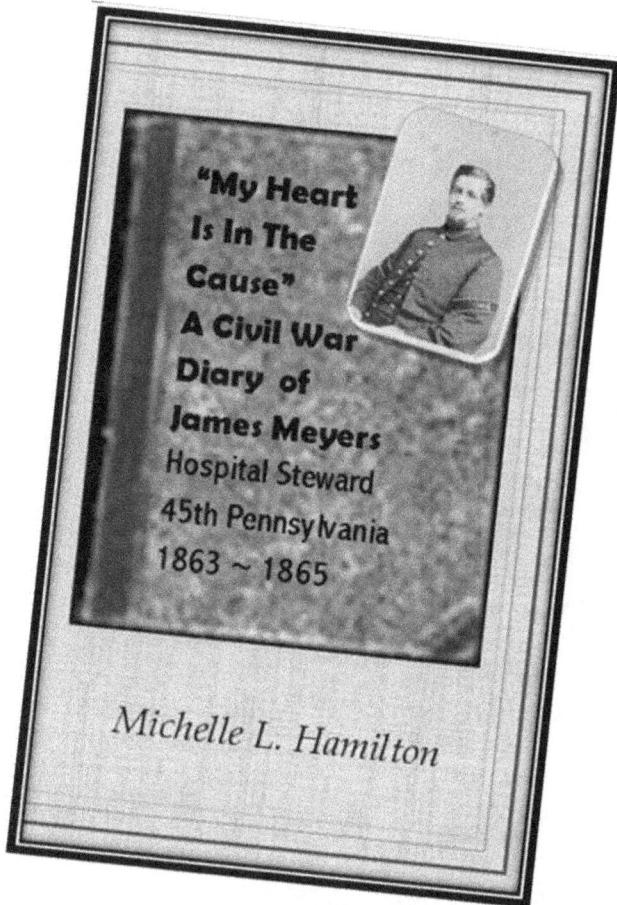

"My Heart
Is In The
Cause"
A Civil War
Diary of
James Meyers
Hospital Steward
45th Pennsylvania
1863 ~ 1865

Michelle L. Hamilton

James A. Meyers

Hospital Steward

45th Regt Penna Vet Vols

1st Brig. 2nd Div 9th A.C.

Dec 25th 1864

Member of Columbia Lodge 286 A.Y.M[110]

Sunday, 1 January 1865.

The New Year finds me Commissary Steward of Field Hospital 2nd Div 9th Army Corps, before Petersburg VA having also in charge the Medical Supplies of our Brigade (1st).

The day is clear and cold with a high keen wind, in afternoon I visited the regiment and found a letter awaiting me from Dr C—. there is no firing from either side along the line today, both parties seem to respect the day—.

This is my third New Year's day in the Army. I must [illegible] another has come there may be no need for the Army in the field—.

Monday, 2 January 1865.

Opens cold, after a freezing night.

To Brigade Hd Qrs on business with Dr. B—. and then to regiment. The mail is doing better, received letters from SRG and L.T.F.—.

---

[110] Columbia (Pennsylvania) Masonic Lodge 286 Ancient York Masons.

Made out requisitions for the monthly medical supplies.

Tuesday, 3 January 1865.

Overcast and threatening storm. To Corps Hd Quarters to have requisitions approved, in morning—also to the regiment.

Recd letter from S.B.G—

Night closes in with a snow storm. All quiet along the line—

Wednesday, 4 January 1865.

The ground this morning presents a white covering of snow, several inches thick to day is clear and bright.

To the Med Purveyor's at City Point for medical supplies, in morning, and to Brig Hd Qrs & the regiment in afternoon.

Thursday, 5 January 1865.

Growing milder, to Brig Hd Qrs in morning, and to the regiment—stopped for dinner with W.H.P—. recd from home by R. Hall a better pipe & tobacco from Bro WHM—clothing &c also a piece of Bro E.J.M's wedding cake.

I am now fixed for the winter.

Made application for furlough—and don't expect to get it—

An engine on the RRd exploded near our Hospl this afternoon—

Friday, 6 January 1865.

Opens overcast with a little rain—ground is very soft and muddy—proves a very stormy day with heavy rain—

An execution for desertion took place near Division Hd Quarters today.

Saturday, 7 January 1865.

Opens bright with scudding clouds and high wind—

To Brig Hd Quarters, and the regiment—road very muddy— drew clothing.

The sun goes down bright and clear—and the night is cold.

Drew Blouse and Trousers from R.Q.M[111] today.

Sunday, 8 January 1865.

Weather pleasant with indications of another change.

Spent the day quietly in camp—

Dr Webster, left for home—

Dr Oakes 56th Mass assumed charge of Hospital.

Monday, 9 January 1865.

Weather overcast and mild the ground is very soft & muddy.

Everything is very quiet—finished reading Scott's Ivanhoe[112]— was much pleased and interested with it.

Rain sets in about 11 PM.

Tuesday, 10 January 1865.

Opens with rain, which has poured down continually during the past night—. Storm of thunder and lightening in the morning—the first this year.

Wednesday, 11 January 1865.

Clear and pleasant after the storm, which has left much work in repairing works and houses.

---

[111] Regimental Quartermaster
[112] *Ivanhoe* (1820) by Sir Walter Scott

Rode to the regiment in the morning.

Thursday, 12 January 1865.

Beautifully clear and mild. A flag of truce is up today, causing general quiet on the line.

Rode to Corps Hd Qrs, the regiment & 36th Mass is afternoon.

Genl Butler's[113] removal is creating some talk.

Friday, 13 January 1865.

The weather continues mild & springlike, but wears an indication of change.

The mail brings me two letters this A.M.

"Stoney" one my old Hospital attendants captured June 18th '64 returned last evening and visited me today.

Recd through Mrs Husband at City Point Sunday good things from the Philada friends—

Saturday, 14 January 1865.

Clear with high northwind—the weather growing colder—

To Brigade Hd Quarters in morning—

Wrote to A.M.C and L.S.J—The mail today brings me nothing but the "Spy" of last week—

---

[113] Major General Benjamin Butler (1818-1893) was removed from command of the Army of the James on January 8, 1865 after failing to attack Petersburg, Virginia as ordered by General Ulysses S. Grant. Rather than attack the city of Petersburg, Butler's army got bogged down in an area known as Bermuda Hundred.

Sunday, 15 January 1865.

Clear and pleasant—the day is very quiet—remained quietly in my quarters, finished reading Scotts "Old Mortality,"[114] was not much pleased with it—

Wrote to Dr Christ in evening.

Monday, 16 January 1865.

Bright and pleasant—spent the day quietly in camp—many and varied rumors are afloat, mostly speaking of peace.

Recd letter from S.A.M & the Press, by mail.

Tuesday, 17 January 1865.

Partially overcast with high cold wind in afternoon—.

A salute in honor of the fall of Fort Fisher was fired today.

Rode to the regiment this afternoon.

The death of Hon 'Edw' Everett[115] is announced in this evening's papers—.

Wednesday, 18 January 1865.

Weather mild.

Remained quiet in camp all day.

Thursday, 19 January 1865.

Overcast and threatens change.

---

[114] *Old Mortality* (1816) by Sir Walter Scott

[115] Edward Everett (1794-1865) is considered to be one of the greatest orators of the 19th century. Everett had a long and distinguished career as a U.S. Representative, U.S. Senator, Governor of Massachusetts, and ambassador to the United Kingdom. He is best remembered today for delivering the oration at the dedication of the National Cemetery at Gettysburg, Pennsylvania, November 19, 1863.

Rode to regiment in afternoon Dr Snow returned this P.M.

Friday, 20 January 1865.

Overcast and growing milder.

Changed [illegible] from Commissary & received Courser, also Curran in cookery—

Remained quiet in camp—more cannonading along the line than usual today.

We have rumors of a move or change of place for our Corps. Finished Scott's "Peveril of the Peak,"[116] liked it much.

Saturday, 21 January 1865.

A stormy day, rain, sleet and high wind—.

To Brig Hd Quarters in morning & got a through pelting by the storm. Mail brings me letters from S.R.G and E.B.G— wrote to S.A.M E.T.M. EBG & S.R.G.

Sunday, 22 January 1865.

A damp foggy day, spent quietly in camp—

The mail brings me nothing but the "Press"

Heavy cannonading on the right during the night.

Monday, 23 January 1865.

Wet and unpleasant—remained in camp all day—

Heavy guns are pounding away on the night, the gunboats seem to have work on hand, the night is very dark and foggy—.

---

[116] *Peveril of the Peak* (1823) by Sir Walter Scott

Tuesday, 24 January 1865.

Opens bright and pleasant, the heavy firing was kept up at intervals during the night—followed by an explosion this A.M.

It is reported that a naval engagement took place in the James last night, resulting in the loss of four vessels on the part of the enemy.

The night is cold with high wind. Made out requisition for medical supplies.

Wednesday, 25 January 1865.

Clear and cold. To Corps Hd Qurs in morning, had requisitions approved & visited J.S. B[illegible], also to the regiment, recd by mail 'The Spy' & 'Press.'

Had a visit from Col C[illegible], Comm'd'g the Brigade, Dr Blackwood & Capt Brown of the Staff.

Thursday, 26 January 1865.

Biting cold with high winds & clouds, remained quiet in camp—

Wrote to S.B.G—

Friday, 27 January 1865.

The weather is more moderate then yesterday.

Went to City Point and drew medical supplies for the ensuing month.

J.S.B—spent the evening with me—.

Saturday, 28 January 1865.

Very cold with high wind.

To Bring Hd Quarters and the regiment, stopped to dinner with J.S.R—recd by mail the Press, & letter from WH.M.

Sunday, 29 January 1865.

Opens bright and cold with high wind. Dr Blackwood started home on furlough, Dr Bliss 51ˢᵗ N.Y.V.V. takes his place.

Weather moderated in afternoon, & the evening is bright & pleasant.

J.S.B—spent the afternoon with me.

Monday, 30 January 1865.

Opens bright clear and pleasant and proves a fine day.

Visited the signal tower near "Birney" Station & had a view of the country, received a letter from L.T.F.—. spent the evening at Cribbage with Stew Hill, 9ᵗʰ N.H. and beat him 6 out of 10 games—.

Had a visit from Col Canth Comm'd'g the Brigade & Capt Ames of the Staff—

Dr Snow has gone to Div Hd Quarters & Dr Oakes is again in charge of Hospital.

Tuesday, 31 January 1865.

Mild and pleasant, spent the morning hunting rabbits, and the afternoon quietly in Camp—Considerable cannonading through the day, more than is usual now.

A report is current to-night that Alex Stephens & four other prominent "Rebs" came over this evening & were taken to City Point in a special train that lay on "Meade Station."

There is much stir in Hospl tonight, a sudden order to the ship the sick has come, an attack from the enemy is expected.

Wednesday, 1 February 1865.

The new month opens mild and springlike, very few patients remain in hospital nearly all having been shipped over night.

To the regiment in the morning and received letters & a package from home, per J. Heck.

The day is very quiet not a gun to be heard.

Wrote home in evening.

There are indications of a movement on foot.

Thursday, 2 February 1865.

Mild and pleasant with indications of a change of weather.

Recd a letter from sister Lou M—[117] enclosing photograph.

Spent the day quietly on Camp—.

Friday, 3 February 1865.

Overcast with slight fall of sleet and rain.

Remained quietly in Camp all day—

Saturday, 4 February 1865.

Opens unexpectedly bright and pleasant, mild and springlike—rode to the regiment & saw some of the recently returned boys. The mail brings me 3 of Scotts works.

The night is beautifully bright and moonlight, a lively cannonade and mortar practice is in operation, making a splendid sight and causing rolling thunder among the woods and hills along the Appomattox.

---

[117] "Sister Lou" is likely the wife of Edward J. Meyers.

Sent my warrant & a couple of books home by W.H.P—he starts tomorrow.

Wrote sister Lou this evening—Intelligence of the passage by Congress of the Amendment to the Constitution abolishing slavery was received today, thus gradually step by step in advance—and America will be <u>free</u>[118]

Sunday, 5 February 1865.

Opens overcast—a high cool wind during the day—& a clear night a movement is on foot troops are moving and flying hospital will be sent out.

Monday, 6 February 1865.

Partially overcast and cold.   To Corps Hd Quarters & the regiment in morning and the med Purveyors & City Point in afternoon—Heavy and continuous firing far on the left was distinctly heard through the afternoon and now (12 PM.) is still kept up—evidently a desperate fight is underway— rumors of success & the occupation of the [illegible] side railroad reach us but nothing official yet—.[119]

Tuesday, 7 February 1865.

Opens with a driving storm of rain and sleet, heavy cannonading on the left was plainly heard at noon—rumors are prevalent but lack official character.

---

[118] January 31, 1865 the Thirteenth Amendment, abolishing slavery and indentured servitude in the United States, passed the U.S. House of Representatives.

[119] Battle of Hatcher's Run, Virginia, fought on February 5-7, 1865, between the Union forces of Major General Andrew A. Humphreys (1810-1883) and Major General Gouverneur K. Warren (1830-1882) against Confederate forces of Major General John B. Gordon (1832-1904). Even though the Confederates where able to stop the Union advance, the Battle of Hatcher's Run allowed the Union to extend its siege works.

5.15 P.M. The storm continues & firing sometimes heavy has been heard at intervals all day, just now the thundering of Artillery is loud & continuous, a rumor of the death of Gen Warren is prevalent—

Wednesday, 8 February 1865.

Overcast, thawing and muddy roads—clearing off bright and cold in afternoon—the night is bright & clear.

The news from our left continue vague & uncertain.

Thursday, 9 February 1865.

Cold with strong wind.

Rode to regiment, in morning & saw our new Asst Surg Iddings.

Recd letter from L.T.F & the Press

Friday, 10 February 1865.

Bright & clear, yet cold, remained quietly in Camp—recd a letter from & wrote to S.R.G—.

We have little reliable news stirring.

Saturday, 11 February 1865.

Clear and pleasant—

To Brigade Hd Quarters & the regiment in morning, no mail in & consequently no letters. Wrote to L.T.F. in evening.

Sunday, 12 February 1865.

Clear and cold, with a high N.W-wind, blowing a gale and trying our old Comrades cross to their utmost—.

Recd an answered a letter from M.A.C—. Rode to regiment in afternoon. Dr Y— goes on furlough to-morrow.

Monday, 13 February 1865.

Opens clear but biting cold, the past night has been one of the coldest of the season.

Our new Asst Surgeon Dr Iddings visited me this afternoon, was much pleased with him—

Spent the day quietly in Camp.

Tuesday, 14 February 1865.

Saint Valentine's day opens cold after a severely cold night—

Visited the regiment in morning, received by mail "The Spy" and a letter from S.B.G—. and wrote to A.M.C— AM.R— and L.S.T in all 14 pages—.

Rebel deserters bring a rumor of the capture of Branchville.

Wednesday, 15 February 1865.

Opens with rain which continues throughout the day—

Thursday, 16 February 1865.

Overcast and mild, the rain has ceased but the roads are in a horrible condition—

Rode to regiment in the afternoon—

Recd by mail a letter from E.T.M and The Press.

Stewd—Rodings U.S.A— reported at this Hospital for duty to day—quarters with me to-night—

Friday, 17 February 1865.

Overcast and cheerless—rain through the day—received by mail a letter & pipe from E.T.M—

In evening wrote to E.T.M.

Everything is very quiet—roads bad and all dull

Saturday, 18 February 1865.

Opens clear and bright, mild and pleasant, quite a contrast to the weather of the past week, to the regiment and Brig Hd Quarters in AM.

Sunday, 19 February 1865.

Beautifully clear and pleasant, had a visit from Capt Eyde and J.S.B—, we visited the lookout tower & had a fine view of Petersburg & vicinity

Spent the remainder of the day quietly in Camp—

Monday, 20 February 1865.

Mild, clear, and pleasant. Rode to regiment in morning—

By mail received "The Press" and notice of the death of Dr Wm Breed of Philada—

Dr Snow returned to the charge of the Hospital again today.

Wrote to S.B.G—Indianapolis Ind

Tuesday 21 February 1865.

Bright and pleasant—remained quietly in camp—having almost nothing to do I can scarce content myself.

The news of the capture of Charleston[120] &c elicit much joyfulness a salute was fired in honor of it.

With the new H.S—R—things do not go so pleasantly.

---

[120] Charleston, South Carolina surrendered to Brigadier General Alexander Schimmelfiennig on February 18, 1865.

Wednesday, 22 February 1865.

The anniversary of the birth of Washington—mild pleasant and overcast—A national salute was fired at noon in honor of the day—Considerable cannonading in morning with some loss in our 1st Division—

Rode to regiment & receive from home through WHP—letters, vest &c.

The mail gives me only the Spy of 18th—.

Thursday, 23 February 1865.

Opens mild with rain—

Everything is dull and quiet. I am having a severe attack of "ennui".[121] In camp all day.

Recd letter from Mat C—

The night sets in wet, and the rain pours down steadily.

The paymasters are stirring.

Friday, 24 February 1865.

Overcast and mild, but the rain has ceased—

News of the capture of Wilmington have been received, and one hundred shotted guns fired in honor of the event, at 4 PM.

Deserters are coming in rapidly—.

J.S.B—spent the evening with me—

Recd a long letter from S.R.G—

---

[121] French for weariness, lack of interest, boredom.

Saturday, 25 February 1865.

Wet and unpleasant, rode to Brig Hd Qrs and regiment this A.M. received by mail a letter from L.S.T- and the "Press."

Desertions from the enemy continue frequent, twenty one came into our Brigade last night.

Wrote to S.A.M and SRG-

Sunday, 26 February 1865.

Opens overcast but clears up mild and pleasant with wind.

Monday, 27 February 1865.

Mild, clear and pleasant—

Made monthly requisition for med supplies.

To the front & Corps Hd Quarters in afternoon

Tuesday, 28 February 1865.

Wet and unpleasant, quiet with little doing—

In camp all day—

Wednesday, 1 March 1865.

Overcast and unpleasant, to the Med Purveyor's for supplies in morning, and the regiment in evening, the regt was paid to-night, received my pay to Dec 31ˢᵗ 1864. (132.00) We were paid by Maj Haviland

I turn in to-night early, feeling very unwell.

Thursday, 2 March 1865.

Opens with rain, which continues throughout the day, am feeling very unwell.

Friday, 3 March 1865.

Overcast and mild with a little rain. Get up this morning feeling much better.

In camp all day—

Saturday, 4 March 1865.

Opens with a very heavy storm of wind and rain. Clears up fine and closes bright and pleasant. To Brig Hd Qrs and the regiment in A.M.

Wrote to Bro W.H.M—and enclosed paymaster T.P. Hairland's check upon Asst Treas U.S. at N.Y. no 84, dated Mar 1st 1865, for one hundred dollars ($100.00) to my order, and by me made payable to W.H.M—.

Sunday, 5 March 1865.

Bright and pleasant.

Rode out with Jake B. in afternoon & wrote to M.A.C in evening.

Monday, 6 March 1865.

Bright and pleasant.

Quiet and in Camp all day, recd letter from S.R.G— and wrote to L.S.T—

Tuesday, 7 March 1865.

Bright and very pleasant.

Rode to Brig Hd Qrs and the regiment in morning.

Recd by mail the Spy & one other paper—

11.30 P.M. The bells of P—g are ringing the alarm loudly and a large fire may be distinctly seen in direction of the city, the night is calm and a bright moon shinning.

Wednesday, 8 March 1865.

Opens overcast and proves a rainy day—quiet in camp throughout the day.

The mail brings me letters from L.T.F. and SAM—unusually good fortune—Wrote to SA.M.

The night is wet and unpleasant.

Thursday, 9 March 1865.

Opens after a night of heavy rain, with a dense fog—

One year ago our regiment reorganized after 30 days furlough—

The day is warm with occasionally gleams of sunshine.

Wrote to L.T.F.—

Friday, 10 March 1865.

Opens overcast with N.W. wind followed by a driving storm of rain and sleet—making all out doors very disagreeable— finished reading Scott's "Heart of Mid Lorthian"[122]

The day closes bright but somewhat colder—the mail brings me the Press

Saturday, 11 March 1865.

The storm has passed by again & the day is clear and cool, yet pleasant—

Made my Saturday morning trip to Brig Hd Qrs & the regiment, by mail recd letter from A.M.C dated Jan'y 1ˢᵗ, answered it & wrote to S.R.G—

---

[122] *The Heart of Midlothian* (1818) by Sir Walter Scott

Dr Snow goes to Div Hd Qrs again—and we have Dr Oakes again in charge of hospital.

Sunday, 12 March 1865.

Beautifully clear and bright. Remained quiet in Camp all day—

The mail is favoring me again, letter from S.A.M & S.B.G— also some photo's from S.R.G—which I had sent for.

Monday, 13 March 1865.

Bright and pleasant—

To the regiment in afternoon. Had a visit from Gen Curtin & Dr Blackburn—The mail brings me only the Press—

Wrote to M.A.C—

Tuesday, 14 March 1865.

Mild and pleasant, with indications of a coming storm.

Order's to clear hospital, sent sick to City Point in evening and received many others from regiments.

To be ready to move at a moments notice are our orders—

Wednesday, 15 March 1865.

Overcast with warm wind.

The indications of a coming movement continued. Sutlers and surplus baggage are ordered to the rear.

Rain in afternoon but the sun set bright. By mail received papers, also package from S.A.M—wrote to S.A.M in evening.

Rain during the night.

Thursday, 16 March 1865.

Overcast with high and mild wind—the moving alarm seems passing by.

By mail received four letters two of them a month old.

The day is made very unpleasant by the sand driven by the high wind—heavy storm of rain at night.

J.S.B— spent the evening with me—Wrote to SRG—

Friday, 17 March 1865.

After a wild stormy night, St. Patrick's day opens bright and clear, with the temperature much lower than yesterday.

Wrote to ET.M.

Saturday, 18 March 1865.

Beautifully clear and pleasant to Brig Hd Qrs & regiment in morning took dinner with Adjr Dickinson, exchanged photos with Gen Curtin.

New troops are daily arriving the 21st Penna passed today.

Sunday, 19 March 1865.

Serenely beautiful and bright.

Remained quiet in camp all day, recd letter from M.A.C & wrote to S.B.G—. Attended divine service in Chapel of U.S.C.C. at Meade station in evening.

Five months more from today, half my <u>conscripted</u> time is passed.

Monday, 20 March 1865.

Clear and uncomfortably warm—To City Point by R.Rd in morning, returned at 1 P.M. Flies are appearing quite plentiful.

Heavy artillery firing in afternoon with but little or no damage to us.

Tuesday, 21 March 1865.

Opens overcast, warm and sultry. Rode to the regiment in morning.

By mail received letter from M.A.C—.

A fine refreshing rain in afternoon, vegetation is rapidly pushing forward, the fruit trees are already in blossom.

A visit from A.A.Y—in afternoon.

Wednesday, 22 March 1865.

After a rainy night, the day appears bright and clear with high winds, the temperature much reduced since yesterday.

Quiet in camp all day, the high wind blows the sand around in such a manner as to make out of doors unpleasant.

Rec and answered letter from A.M.C also recd a letter from L.S.T—.

Thursday, 23 March 1865.

Bright and clear, with high wind, blowing great clouds of sand about.

To the regiment in morning & recd by mail last week's Spy.

All remains quiet along the line. Sent my overcoat home today by express from Balto—

Friday, 24 March 1865.

Partially overcast, somewhat cooler with high west wind.

Recd by mail "The Press" and letter from S.R.G— also letter from LT.F.

Wrote to LS.T—and to M.A.C enclosing to the latter $3.00.

Saturday, 25 March 1865.

Aroused before day by heavy fire in front of line occupied by our 1ˢᵗ Div which proved to be an attack by the enemy, who surprised & carried Ft Steadman and made some headway but met a most severe repulse, at the hands of the 3ʳᵈ Div (Penna) & the batteries were driven back to there own lines with a loss of about 4000—while our loss will not exceed 500, we captured several thousand prisoners the enemies loss in killed was very large. Our division was not engaged, but our hospital is filled with wounded Johnnies.

What seemed at first to be a loss to us, proved a great victory, our camp at first was thrown in uproar & pack up was the order.

The day was overcast & chilly, and closes much more satisfactorily than it commenced.

At Corps Hd Qrs in afternoon I saw seven captured flags, trophies of today's work.

Sunday, 26 March 1865.

Opens cold and unpleasant, but in afternoon clears up and grows somewhat pleasant.

Many of our wounded prisoners are being sent away, and evening finds only the severest cases remaining, two rebel majors are amongst those who have died here.

The majority of the wounds are very severe, many limbs have been amputated.

Rode to regiment in afternoon, and recd per Lt C. Roch[123] Co K. several articles & a letter from home.

---

[123] 2ⁿᵈ Lieutenant Charles H. Koch was recruited from Lancaster County and mustered into service on October 5, 1861. Koch was promoted from

The day closes clear and quiet.

Monday, 27 March 1865.

Clear and pleasant, to the Med Purveyor's & City Point this A.M. drew Med Supplies for month of April.

A great stir is being made in the Army. Sheridan's Cavalry crossed the A—[124] this A.M. and went into camp to the rear of Div Hd Qrs, the raid are creating much comment.

A busy afternoon overhauling & repacking Med Supplies in readiness for forward announcements.

A.A.Y— stays with me to-night, starts home to-morrow taking with the remains of Lt W.H Child—. I send by him letter to S.A.M. & package of old letters for storage & safe keeping.

Tuesday, 28 March 1865.

Overcast and sultry, up early & assisted A.A.Y— in shipping C—s remains, then rode to regiment & in company with W.H.P— visited the Cavalry Corps and in the 2nd Mass found Ned B[illegible] formerly of Cola[125] had a very pleasant visit & glad to meet a former schoolmate, the cavalry boys look rough & ready.

Heavy additions of troops are passing to the left everything is in commotion, preparatory to some great and we trust decisive movement. Our hospital is being cleaned, and we are in readiness for our share.

The day closes with indications of a forward movement at early hour, and the sky says rain—.

Corporal to Sergeant on March 28, 1862. On January 2, 1865, Koch was promoted to 2nd Lieutenant; he received his final promotion to 1st Lieutenant on June 8, 1865. Koch mustered out with the regiment on July 17, 1865.

[124] Appomattox River

[125] Columbia, Pennsylvania

By mail recd letter from Sister Lou.

Wednesday, 29 March 1865.

Partially overcast and quite warm.

Another trip to City Point and Med Purveyor's, drawing supplies, Instruments &c, and turned in Dr B's mess chest, had a warm ride returned at noon.

Remained quietly in Camp the remainder of the day.

Rumors of an extensive move of the Army on the left and of successes there are current, but nothing yet reliable.

Wrote to S.R.G— in evening—

About 10 P.M. a most furious cannonade was opened extending from the A— to Fort Hell it was a grand & terrific sight, the most so, of the kind I have ever witnessed, dozens of shells were flying thro' the air at one time, by midnight almost all had ceased, one man, a private of 45th P.V.V. was recd in our hospital wounded during the bombardment, the 1st Div suffered more heavily.

Rain sets in before 12 P.M.

Thursday, 30 March 1865.

Opens with rain which continues until 4 P.M.

Heavy firing is to be heard far to the left, and doubtless an important engagement is in progress there. Dr Snow returned to the charge of the hospital yesterday.

Remained quietly in Camp all day. The night sets in clear with a bright new moon.

Wrote to L.T.F—.

Friday, 31 March 1865.

Contrary to our anticipations, the day opens with a steady rain, which continues for some hours, followed by high wind and scudding clouds. Remained in Camp all day, recd letter from S.R.G—

The Hospl fund for the current month shows well, footed it up today.

The day closes with a bright sun. Had a visit from Dr Y— and Adjt Dickinson this P.M.—

At intervals today heavy firing on the left was heard, but no reliable news can be obtained, tho' many rumors pro & con are afloat.

Saturday, 1 April 1865.

Opens bright clear and pleasant to Brig Hd Qrs & the regiment in A.M. met our new Chaplin (Rev Gast)[126] was very well pleased with him.

Our new Corps Med Director Dr Dalton visited hospital today.

Made semi monthly report of Med Supplies on hand today.

The night is bright and clear about 10 o'clock heavy artillery firing is opened on the left, in our front all is quiet.

Sunday, 2 April 1865.

Partially overcast and very sultry.

Aroused about midnight by rapid firing and the noise of a charge on the line of our corps, heavy firing could be heard on the direction of the Army of the James, also on our left.

---

[126] Chaplin Frederick A. Gast mustered into service during the spring of 1865, he was mustered out of service with 45th PA Veteran Volunteers on July 17, 1865.

Before long it was evident there was a general attack by our forces and by daylight the wounded of our Corps began to arrive then came news of successes in all quarters, the forts in front of Fort Hell & vicinity in our possession.

Throughout the day the firing & fighting was most stubborn, large fires in Pb'g were plainly visible

We have in Hospital more than 300 wounded, amongst them Capt Chessman[127] comm'd'g our regt who loses his right leg. Major Peckham A A.G of our Brig is wounded mortally. Capt Eyde[128]—is a prisoner.

Am hurried off tonight in charge of a train of wounded to City Point.

The night is comparatively quiet.

Monday, 3 April 1865.

Opens overcast, after a short nap daylight finds me at C— P— return to the field by 6.30 and soon after learn the glorious intelligence of the occupation of Pb'g and following it the news of the fall of Richmond. Thus at length the

---

[127] Captain Rowland C. Chessman was recruited from Centre County and mustered into service in Company A on August 20, 1861. Chessman was promoted to 1st Sergeant on September 25, 1862 and was promoted to 2nd Lieutenant on March 18, 1863. On September 29, 1864, Chessman was made Captain of Company F. Chessman was wounded twice the Battle of Blue Springs, Kentucky on October 10, 1863 and at Petersburg, Virginia on June 18, 1864. On September 30, 1864, Chessman was captured by the Confederates. Upon his return to the regiment, Chessman was transferred from Company F. Chessman was made a Brevet Major on April 2, 1865 following the amputation of his right leg. Recovering from his injury, Chessman mustered out with the regiment on July 17, 1865.

[128] Captain Edgar Eyde was recruited from Lancaster County and mustered into service in Company K on August 22, 1861. Eyde was promoted to Corporal on November 28, 1862 and was promoted to Sergeant on November 24, 1863. On July 9, 1864, Eyde was promoted to 2nd Lieutenant on January 2, 1865. Eyde was wounded at Petersburg, Virginia on July 30, 1864. Eyde returned to the regiment and was mustered out of service on July 17, 1865.

XXXiege is ended successfully. We pursue the flying enemy and our hospital is under marching orders.

Move about 4 P.M. passing thro' the famed "Cockade City" a large portion of which shows the effects of our guns upon it entered the enemy's lines near the scene of the mine failure of July 30th the 1st Div of our Corps were the first to enter the City & are to garrison it.

Thousands of prisoners are being sent off in two squads I saw 7000. Pushing thro' P— we march about 6 miles beyond toward Lynchburg & camp for the night, again we are in active field service.

This day will be a day of rejoicing at home, the Rebellion is rapidly passing away.

Tuesday, 4 April 1865.

Up and ready to march at 5 A.M. but, make but little progress until late in afternoon, then pull out steadily until about 11 P.M. Camp and turn in at 12.30.

We today crossed & recrossed the South Side RRd several times following nearly parallel to it.

Camp at night about 18 miles from Pb'g. The day is warm.

Wednesday, 5 April 1865.

The weather continues favorable & everything progresses well—continue our march passing Ford Station early in the day. Camped at night near Wellsville.

Thursday, 6 April 1865.

Opens overcast with slight fall of rain, lay quiet until about 3 P.M & then resumed the march camping at night at Nottaway C.H.

Friday, 7 April 1865.

Reached Burkeville about 2 P.M. & immediately established hospital and received wounded from 6th & 2nd Corps, filling up rapidly—Thousands of rebel prisoners & many guns arrived here today, among them Gen Ewell[129] & six other guns.

Saturday, 8 April 1865.

The weather continues favorable & the sound of heavy fighting may be heard at the front.

Very busy—have in all about 400 men—

Sunday, 9 April 1865.

Still at Burkeville—rec'd our mail with news from home, the good work goes on & prisoners continue arriving. We are living in a great measure off the country, hospital affairs work well—

The night is cold & unpleasant

Monday, 10 April 1865.

Opens with rain and proves a wet day—

The official news of the surrender of Lee & his Army reached us today, this is the crowning stroke & creates great joy.[130]

The events of the past 10 days seem unreal, and now that the long looked for event has arrived it can scarce be credited.

The railroad was opened thro from City Point today.

---

[129] Lieutenant General Richard S. Ewell was captured with his troops after surrendering after being defeated at the Battle of Sailor's Creek on April 6, 1865.

[130] General Robert E. Lee (1807-1870) surrounded the Army of Northern Virginia to General Ulysses S. Grant at Appomattox Court House on April 9, 1865.

Tuesday, 11 April 1865.

At Burkeville VA

Wednesday, 12 April 1865.

At Burkeville VA

Thursday, 13 April 1865.

At Burkeville VA

Friday, 14 April 1865.

Partially clear, sun warm and sultry—.

Still at Burkeville VA

Saturday, 15 April 1865.

Opens with rain and proves a very wet day—the week has been a rainy one & the roads are in horrible condition. Paroled rebels are almost as plentiful amongst us as our own men, they are scattering for their homes.

A rumor stating that President Lincoln has been assassinated in Washington is current this P.M. it seems too horrible too be true, and I surely trust it may prove utterly false.

Sunday, 16 April 1865.

Beautifully clear and bright.

Quiet in Camp all day, wrote to E.T.M—.

Monday, 17 April 1865.

Clear and warm—

The official report of the death of our noble President is being read to the troops today—creating much deep felt sorrow and indignation, we had until now hoped that the rumor might prove false. Alas! It has proved but too true.

Sold my mule and bought a horse, rode to Farmville (18 miles) & visited the regiment and some others camped there.

Visited a large Reb Hospl located at F. under charge of Surg F[illegible] C.S.A

Tuesday, 18 April 1865.

Spent the day at Farmville which I find a beautifully located town, the best looking place I have seen in VA yet the mark of war is on it.

Visited the locality of the high bridge on the Lynchburg RRd

In the evening long visitation of Dr B— I attended an impromptu concert at the F- hotel by some of the musicians of our Brigade & was well pleased.

Wednesday, 19 April 1865.

Clear and warm, in morning returned from regiment to the Hospital at Burkeville Junction.

This is the day appointed for the funeral of our murdered President, and is being very generally observed, labor is suspended, a salute of 21 minute guns fired at noon and all flags are at half mast, appropriate addresses are being made to the troops assembled and bands and drum corps are sounding the funeral dirge, everyone feels the loss his own and is sad and sorrowful, to think that at the [illegible] of his glory and prosperity our loved and tried President should thus be slain—O higher than many rules, and will guide us through. My tent was robbed to-night of about $20.00 worth of clothing.

Thursday, 20 April 1865.

Overcast, with heavy rain late in the day, received sudden marching orders this A.M. broke Camp and started for City Point & it is said thence we go to Washington

By hard work, the roads being in bad condition we made about 18 miles by 10 P.M. we go back over the same road that we came

Turned in after midnight.

Friday, 21 April 1865.

Opens overcast, aroused at four A.M. with orders to be ready to move at 5— after making very good time, we go into camp 18 miles from Petersburg at nightfall, another rain storm but not so severe as that of last night.

Saturday, 22 April 1865.

Starting ahead of the train this A.M. Steward Benton & myself reached Petersburg about 11.30 A.M. and spent the day about the City which has changed much since our first entrance.

Met a number of our officers recently returned from prison & awaiting the regiment.

The day is bright and hot. Camped at night inside the old Rebel line of works opposite Fort Steadman

A cold night.

Sunday, 23 April 1865.

Clear with high cold wind. Visited Fort Steadman and the surrounding lines, and the scene of the fight of March 25th 1865.

Marched to the vicinity of City Point and camped on the banks of the Appomattox to await transportation to Washington.

Monday, 24 April 1865.

Bright clear and warm, drew rations for the remainder of the month. Our brigade came in this A.M. visited the regiment & Brig Hd Qrs. Had my horse shod in afternoon.

Tuesday, 25 April 1865.

The shipment of troops of our Corps continues shipping from C—P—. we await transportation.

Wednesday, 26 April 1865.

Weather hot and ground dry and very dusty.

Still awaiting transportation. The brigade leaves tonight.

Thursday, 27 April 1865.

Still at C— P— and weather hot.

The brigade leaves to-night. Surg B— left for W—[131] today.

Friday, 28 April 1865.

Still at C. P—.

Med officers & horses left this A.M. sent my horse with them. A salute of 1000 guns was fired this P.M. in honor of Grant's successes over Johnston.[132]

---

[131] Washington, D.C.

[132] General Joseph E. Johnston surrendered the Army of the Tennessee and all Confederate forces still active in North Carolina, South Carolina, Georgia, and Florida to General William T. Sherman.

Saturday, 29 April 1865.

Ambulance trains of 1ˢᵗ and 3ʳᵈ Divs are shipping, no move for us yet.

Rain in evening

Sunday, 30 April 1865.

After the rain proves a beautiful and pleasant day—

In morning took a pleasant walk thro' the woods around and visited Broadway landing, on the Appomattox.

Monday, 1 May 1865.

Opens clear and warm, to City Point & drew rations for all hands this A.M. returned to Camp at noon & received very unexpected orders to move, embarked on board steamer Manhattan and about 4 P.M. bid good bye to City Point and Army of Potomac.

Tuesday, 2 May 1865.

After a restless night morning finds us steaming up the Chesapeake bay, the day is cool & overcast, after a pleasant run we reach Alexandria at about 8 P.M. went ashore had a stroll around town, returned to the boat & quartered on board for the night.

Wednesday, 3 May 1865.

Up at daybreak and unloaded our baggage then moved thro' the City and went into Camp to the rear of Fort Lyon & near Brigade Hd Quarters.

Rode to town in afternoon.

Thursday, 4 May 1865.

Lying quietly in Camp, in a pleasant spot. To town and drew rations from Capt Alley—C.S.

Friday, 5 May 1865.

Weather pleasant, another trip to town today on business.

Saturday, 6 May 1865.

Weather growing warmer, during the past night we had a heavy storm of thunder and lighting.

Obtained a pass and visited Washington, found my old friend Matth C— all right, & with him visited many of the notable places, amongst others the National Capitol.

Friday, 12 May 1865.

After a night of storm, the severest we have experienced for some time the day breaks clear but quite cold. This is the anniversary of the great battle of Spottsylvania and brings many sad remembrances with it.

In company with Stewd Lister 58th Mass I visited Mt Vernon, & the tomb of Washington, was much pleased and happy to be able to visit this spot dear to every true American,—the day was charming and the ride in every way delightful—

In evening visited the regiment and recd by mail letters from E.T.M & S.R.G.—. There was a grand illumination by all the troops around commencing with our Brigade—in honor of the battle anniversary.

Tuesday, 23 May 1865.

At Washington D.C. witnessing the Grand Review of the Army, a glorious day for both civilian and soldier, and are full of proud feelings to cheer who followed the old flag, how proudly the boys step out, the Avenue will never see another such sight, our old Corps leads the Infantry [illegible]— return to camp at night.

Wednesday, 24 May 1865.

Again in Washington seeing the triumphal march of Sherman and his men, meet with many old friends and comrades, return to Alexandria very tired sold my horse to B.F. Brunner & footed it to Camp, learn that I can be mustered out at once and go to work on papers tomorrow.

Thursday, 25 May 1865.

Spent the day at work on muster out rolls, to find on going to Div Hd Qrs that they are wrong, must begin again and do so tonight.

Friday, 26 May 1865.

A very wet day—

A Citizen once more. I was this day mustered out of service, near Alexandria Virginia by the mustering officer of the division.

Am the first enlisted man of 9th Corps mustered out under the order for disbanding the Army.

Bid goodbye to my friends in 11th & 6th New Hampshire & 36 Mass regm—

Saturday, 27 May 1865.

Start for home, bid good bye to my old comrades of the 45th with feelings of mingled joy & sadness.

By boat to Washington, met M.A.C and spent the remainder of the day with him. After much delay get off finally by rail about 8 P.M. a half of an hour at Baltimore and then on to York PA where I turn in at midnight.

Sunday, 28 May 1865.

A pleasant day, spent quietly with Aunt H's family at York.

Monday, 29 May 1865.

Leave York for Hbg[133] at 12M after very little delay receive my final payment and start for home at 3 P.M.

Home again! And very unexpectedly to the friends here. Numerous of my old comrades who have preceded me, all calling to hear news from the boys left at Alexandria.

---

[133] Harrisburg, Pennsylvania

Appendix
Medical History of the Forty-Fifth Regiment

At the time of organization of the regiment at Camp Curtin the Medical Staff was composed of George L. Potter, of Bellefonte, Pa., surgeon, and Theodore S. Christ, of Lewisburg, Pa., assistant surgeon. W. Godfrey Hunter was promoted from private Company A to hospital steward, November 26th, 1861.

Dr. Potter, who was a well educated, capable medical officer, resigned from the service August 1st, 1862. Assistant Surgeon Theodore S. Christ succeeded Surgeon Potter, his promotion dating from August 4th, 1862.

Charles S. Styer succeeded Dr. Christ as assistant surgeon, with muster dating from August 1st, 1862. He was a competent officer, well liked by the men and officers and remained with the regiment until promoted Surgeon United States Volunteers, January 12th, 1863.

Robert R. Wiestling joined the regiment as second assistant surgeon, his muster dating from August 13th, 1862.

Dr. Wiestling was present and on duty during the Battle of South Mountain, September 14th, 1862, was taken sick and went to hospital with typhoid fever. Being broken in health he resigned from the service February 22d, 1863. Dr. Wiestling gave promise of making a useful medical officer and his loss was regretted.

W.S. Yundt was mustered as assistant surgeon, February 23d, 1863, and resigned May 18th, 1865. Dr. Yundt was a genial man and soon made many friends in the command. He was capable as a medical officer and should have been promoted to surgeon on the resignation of Surgeon Christ. Unfortunately, however, Governor Curtin could not be induced to accede to the recommendation for promotion of Dr. Yundt, which was strongly urged by Colonel John I. Curtin and others, and instead, after the war and field service were ended, promoted a stranger to hold the position for the few remaining weeks, thereby depriving Dr. Yundt of an honor which was justly his due. Naturally, the doctor resigned.

John K. Maxwell mustered as assistant surgeon, March 3d, 1863.

Dr. Maxwell was a man with a strong personality; somewhat older than the majority of the officers and men, and with difficulty adjusted himself to his position as second assistant surgeon. He was, however, an efficient medical officer and honest in the performance of his duties. He was severely injured near Milldale, Miss., from which he never fully recovered. He resigned August 27th, 1864.

The vacancy occasioned by the resignation of Assistant Surgeon Maxwell was filled by the appointment of C. Edward Iddings, who was mustered out with the regiment July 17th, 1865.

F.B. Davidson, who entered the service August 12th, 1864, as assistant surgeon, Second Pennsylvania Cavalry, was transferred and mustered as surgeon of the Forty-fifth, dating from May 27th, 1865.

F.B. Davidson, who entered the service August 12th, 1864, as assistant surgeon, Second Pennsylvania Cavalry, was transferred and mustered as surgeon of the Forty-fifth, dating from May 27th, 1865.

Of the noncommissioned medical staff, Hospital Steward W. Godfrey Hunter was mustered out in September, 1862, to accept promotion as assistant surgeon of another regiment. The vacancy thus occasioned was filled by the promotion of James A. Myers [Sic.], a private of Company B, to be hospital steward, the date of his warrant being September 22d, 1862. Steward Myers remained in this position until May 26th, 1865, when he was discharged by special order of the War Department at Alexandria, Va.

H.D. Deming, private Company G, was promoted to fill the vacancy and mustered out with the regiment.

Unfortunately, the work of writing a regimental history was from various causes delayed, until now after a lapse of more than 45 years, the writer being the only survivor of those of the medical staff who followed the fortunes and participated in the work of our dear old regiment, is called upon to prepare as well as he may something of its medical history. This could have been done so much better by one or more who are no longer with us that I have approached the task with great reluctance. I am, however, doing the best that I can to place on record from the little data at my command and from memory something which I trust may have some interest to the few members of the regiment who survive and possibly to the posterity of those who followed the flag of the Forty-fifth.

Of the work of the Medical Department in the early days and while the regiment was in South Carolina I have no personal knowledge. During this period it appears to have been largely confined to the ordinary routine among the sick, there having been no engagements in which any considerable number were wounded; nor had there been any extended experience such as is acquired only when operating in connection with armies in movements and facing the enemy. So that when the troops under command of General Burnside became a part of the army under General McClellan there was much to be learned by the Medical Staff. Our regiment on reaching Washington, September 6th, 1862, became a part of the Army of the Potomac and as such participated in the Battle of South Mountain, September 14th, 1862. In going into this fight the surgeon and both assistants were with the regiment. This seemed to be considered the proper place for them. However, when the musketry fire opened and the air was full of uncomfortable sounds, Dr. Christ soon realized that—to use his own words—"it is to — hot hear;"

turning to the assistant surgeons, he ordered them to attend to the temporary dressings of the many wounded, sending them a little way down the mountain to a little log house where he established our field hospital. This was not entirely out of range, but on the whole better suited to the work that was in hand, and work it was, for our boys were hard hit. The loss in our regiment alone being about 140 killed and wounded.

The scenes in and about that little log house I cannot describe, but there is one impression gained there and on many subsequent fields that remains with me, and that is with what uncomplaining fortitude the boys bore their sufferings. Patiently they awaited the attention that was so necessary, and patiently and without murmur they met the advance of death.

Our next engagement was three days later at Antietam. Here while the fighting was terrific and the losses of our army great, it was the great good fortune of our regiment to escape with a comparatively small list of killed and wounded, yet there was plenty of work for all.

In October, while encamped at Pleasant Valley, Md., there seemed to be an outbreak of itch about regimental headquarters. Remedies were asked for and used until one day Sumner Pettus, one of the hospital attendants, engaged in washing underclothing for Dr. —, called my attention to a condition which explained the outbreak of itch, as supposed, but which was nothing else than a host of the soldiers' friends or enemies, as you chose, the gentle and close sticking "grayback." Result, no more medicines but an order from headquarters for a general wash up. Boys, do you remember the day when your only suit was hung on the bushes along the creek to dry while you sat in the sun?

Considering all the exposure of this campaign, the general health of the regiment remained good. There was but one death in camp from disease until after reaching Fredericksburg; this was at Waterford, Va.

At Fredericksburg, during the great battle of December 12th, 1862, the field hospital of the division was located in the court house. Here was performed an operation in conservative surgery which at that time was new to us. Surgeon Coggswell of the Twenty-ninth Massachusetts by resection removed a considerable portion of the bone of the upper arm, which had been fractured by a ball, thereby saving the arm. The man was one of our own, whose name I have forgotten. His recovery was rapid. During the siege of Knoxville this same surgeon by resection removed a considerable portion of the lower jaw of one of his men. This was a case of comminuted fracture. This man also made a good recovery.

From Fredericksburg to Newport News, during our stay here, there was a smallpox scare, resulting in a general order for vaccination. It was something to see the first sergeants bringing their men by companies each with a bared arm to receive the virus.

There were a lot of sore arms but no smallpox in the regiment. More than a year later at Petersburg, Va., Quartermaster Sergeant J. Hall Musser developed the only case we had. Prompt isolation and a stay of a couple of months in a tent far away from others and Musser showed up good as new and can to-day answer the roll call for himself.

From Newport News to the Blue Grass of Kentucky, a good climate, good water and good food meant that the hospital had but a few patients. But then came the call to Vicksburg. Joe Johnston was threatening Grant's rear and the old reliable Ninth Corps must go. The good pastures of Kentucky were exchanged for the swamps of the Yazoo, filled with malaria and congestive chill. Then began the fight with disease; hospitals filled and many sick in quarters, taken down with chill in the morning, dead and buried by sundown was the record in some cases.

When Vicksburg was about to fall Sherman with his own and the Ninth Corps was sent after Johnston, each regiment of our corps leaving its regimental hospitals filled with sick in the various regimental camps scattered over miles of the Milldale country. The medical officers accompanied the troops. The writer was left in charge at our camp with 55 sick. The situation was strenuous and a call for help resulted in the sending back of Dr. Maxwell with orders to assume charge of and concentrate the various regimental hospitals.

In order to carry out his instructions Dr. Maxwell, accompanied by the writer, started on a tour of inspection, riding in an ambulance. After visiting the camp of the Seventy-ninth New York and starting homeward, the night pitch dark after a thunder storm, the driver losing the road, the ambulance was upset, resulting in the serious injury of Dr. Maxwell and the breaking of three of his ribs. From this he never fully recovered, although with a signal devotion to duty he continued in the service for a year longer. His ultimate end was undoubtedly hastened by this occurrence.

At last came the welcome order to ship our sick and prepare to leave the Milldale valley of death and go up the river Cairo by boat. On reaching here a large number of new cases were transferred to the hospital boat, then by rail to Covinton, Ky. The seeds of disease sown in Mississippi still pursuing us, another lot of sick was sent to hospital, thence to Camp Park and here the sick multiplied until, when the regiment left for Crab Orchard the hospital in charge of the writer contained 155 patients. Here, also, was the only case of diphtheria which we had in all the years, resulting fatally, as did a number of cases of malarial fever. When ordered to rejoin the regiment the most serious cases were sent to the general hospital at Camp Nelson, the others in ambulances and on foot going to Crab Orchard. Hardly had we reached there when marching orders for East Tennessee came. Reveille at 3 A.M., and march at daylight were orders for September 10th. Again our sick boys had to be left behind, this time in charge of Maxwell. A number of the sick of the Mississippi campaign died in the general hospital, others were discharged for physical disability and a number who had recovered and were enroute to rejoin the regiment were captured on the Clinch Mountain in East Tennessee. Many of these died in Rebel prisons.

After a wearisome march the command entered East Tennessee by way of Cumberland Gap. Here under the influence of a good climate the boys recuperated and were ready for the hard campaign which was before them. November found us in the winter quarters at Lenoirs Station on the East Tennessee and Georgia Railroad. From these comfortable quarters the advent of Longstreet drove us. Then the skirmish at Lenoir and retreat to Knoxville with the hot little fight at Campbells Station on November 16th.

Dr. Christ was now surgeon in chief of brigade, with Dr. Yundt in charge of regiment. The retreat to Knoxville proved disastrous to the medical department in the loss of both brigade medical wagons, with all their much needed stores. Our loss proved our enemy's gain and doubtless many a poor Johnny profited by it.

The siege of Knoxville was now on, with our hospital established in the court house. Day by day the list of wounded increased and day by day our scanty store of medical supplies became less until it became necessary to wash old bandages and use them again, repeating the operation from time to time. Disinfectants, excepting a little bromine, we did not have.

Notwithstanding all this and with the main court room lying full of wounded men, we had but one case of gangrene and that was fatal. Operations, major and minor, were of daily occurrence. Finally the climax came when Longstreet assaulted Fort Sanders, November 29th. Then came the streams of wounded Johnnies who all received the same care and attention as our own wounded. They were simply wounded men requiring help.

In recording the names, etc., of the enemy's wounded, I found one who had been brought in on a stretcher. In reply to my question, he said that he was wounded in both legs below the knees. An examination showed no injury, but simply red marks where he had struck the telegraph wire obstruction in front of the fort, plunging headlong among the dead and wounded in the moat. His imagination had done the rest. A somewhat surprised man was turned over to the provost marshal as a prisoner, while one of his comrades remarked, "Yes! If it hadn't been for that damned telegraph wire, we would have got you," and maybe might have done so.

With the disappearance of Longstreet there was little for the medical department except ordinary routine. The homeward march in January, 1864, after reenlisting was made by men who represented the physical cream of the old regiment, and had little need for the doctor.

The opening of the campaign of 1864 found us bringing up the rear of the Army of the Potomac in its march to the Wilderness. With it, but as yet not an integral part, the Ninth Corps went into the Wilderness fight, with the medical department not well prepared for active field service, so much so that after the fight had opened and the writer was ordered to report to the surgeon in charge of the field hospital for duty, there was only the officer himself to be found and the organization was made subsequently as best it could be. However, it was done, and the hosts of wounded cared for, from this time until the end, almost a year later. There was to be no let up and night and day the work went on. As the long day of May 6th was drawing to a close our hospital was located in the rear of the Sixth Corps, the ground lying full of wounded men. Of a sudden an uproar in our front arose and back came a demoralized brigade. Over us they went and we were between the lines. It was uncomfortable and gave promise of a Rebel prison. Two of my attendants, Jim Stonecypher[134] of Company K, and Van Buren Holliday[135] of Company H, volunteering to stay with me, remained until all were ordered within the lines and the wounded rescued.

At Spotsylvania the medical department was handicapped by a lack of shelter from the cold rain, hundreds of wounded lying

---

[134] Private Jas. Stonecypher was recruited from Columbia, Lancaster County and mustered into service on September 8, 1861. On June 18, 1864, Stonecypher was captured by the enemy. Stonecypher mustered out of service with his company on July 17, 1865.

[135] Private Van Buren Holliday was recruited from Tioga County and mustered into service on September 18, 1861. Holliday was mustered out of service with his company on July 17, 1865.

exposed to the elements. At Cold Harbor or Bethesda Church the field hospital was shelled out of three different locations.

After many privations Petersburg was reached. The siege commenced here with a good base of supplies and plenty of material, division hospitals were set up, the wounded and sick well cared for and from time to time sent to the depot hospitals at City Point, and thence to the north. Dr. Christ was now surgeon in chief if division, Dr. W.R.D. Blackwood, of the Forty-eighth Pennsylvania Volunteers, having succeeded him in charge of brigade.

Dr. Maxwell resigned in August, Dr. Iddings succeeding him and Dr. Christ resigned in October, leaving a vacancy unfilled, as before stated.

These resignations were a distinct loss to both the regiment and the service. They were both experienced and capable officers.

At last came the final assault on Petersburg, where Captain Cheeseman, commanding the regiment, lost his leg and Lieutenant Robb was killed. These casualties at the end seemed doubly hard with home in sight.

Petersburg fell; then the chase after Lee; the surrender; back to Alexandria, then Johnny went marching home to Harrisburg and his final discharge.

In conclusion, I wish to say that wherever the regiment went, or whatever duty it was called to preform, its medical staff was there, always ready for service and winning for itself a recognition from the higher authorities of the Medical Department of the army.

Reader, if you find in what I have written something told that will commend itself, I am content.

JAMES A. MYERS,

Hospital Steward.

From *History of the Forty-Fifth Regiment Pennsylvania Veteran Volunteer Infantry, 1861-1865* edited by Allen D. Albert (Williamsport, PA: Grit Publishing Company, 1912, pg. 317-322).

About The Author

*M*ichelle L. Hamilton has earned her master's degree in history from San Diego State University in 2013. She is a lifelong student of history.

Michelle's other works include: "*I Would Still Be Drowned In Tears*" Spiritualism in Abraham Lincoln White House.

Hamilton currently serves as the manager of the Mary Washington House Museum in Fredericksburg, VA. She is not new to historical house museum as she also worked as a docent at The Whaley House Museum in Old Town San Diego from 2001 until 2006.

She has been a Civil War living historian for the past ten years participating in Civil War living history events around California and Virginia. Additionally she has been a requested speaker at several Civil War Roundtable meetings, radio talk shows and numerous magazine publications including "The Citizen's Companion"

See her list of other publications and request a copy from her website: www.MichelleLHamilton.net

Enjoy her blog at: http://michelle-hamilton.blogspot.com

www.ingramcontent.com/pod-product-compliance
Lightning Source LLC
LaVergne TN
LVHW011226080426
835509LV00005B/340